CM0079569931

DRESSED TO KILL

JAMES BOND
THE SUITED HERO

Ian Fleming

DRESSED TO KILL

JAMES BOND
THE SUITED HERO

Written by

Jay McInerney
Nick Foulkes
Neil Norman
Nick Sullivan

With an Introduction by

Albert R. 'Cubby' Broccoli

Concept, Compilation
& Captions by

Colin Woodhead

Designed by

Auro Lecci

Flammarion
Paris - New York

ISBN: 2-08013-618-6
Numéro d'édition: 1121
Dépôt légal: September 1996

Flammarion
26 rue Racine
75006 Paris

200 Park Avenue South
Suite 1406
New York, N. Y. 10003
USA

Origination by Fotolito Toscana, Florence
Printed in Italy by Baioni Stampa, Rome

ACKNOWLEDGEMENTS

The idea for this book arose from research conducted by Brioni of Rome – James Bond's new tailors for *GoldenEye* – into his previous film wardrobes. Their interest, enthusiasm and expertise contributed greatly to the style and content of the book, and their own enquiries led to the discovery of some extremely rare photographs in Italy, America, Germany and Australia.

Eon Films also had a valuable input into the book and gave access to their archive material. Special thanks must go to Barbara Broccoli, John Parkinson, Gordon Arnell, Amanda Schofield and Meg Simmons, all of whom very patiently put up with and responded to many small requests at a time when they had a major film to launch.

In addition to the writers, thanks also go to Linda Marshall for the photo research; John Hondorich for the copy editing; Graham Rye of the James Bond Fan Club and Dr. Siegfried Tesche of Germany for the use of their archives; Nick Bull of U. I. P. Hammersmith for his photo library; Terry O'Neill for the photographs in Doug Hayward's shop; Richard Channing for keeping a watchful eye on all the style details; Marta Lupo for painstakingly checking all the technical tailoring terms; Jonathan Lipman of Angels & Bermans, who with Lindy Hemming made it all possible in the first place.

A special mention needs to be made of Auro Lecci, the designer of the book, whose personal recollection of the films helped to make this such an enjoyable project.

Colin Woodhead

Encouraged and supported by

Brioni and **EON** PRODUCTIONS

CONTENTS

INTRODUCING
JAMES BOND

Albert R. 'Cubby' Broccoli

I first became aware of James Bond during the late Fifties. Like many thousands of others, I read the James Bond novels voraciously, devouring each new one as it was published, and it did not take me long to realize that they would make an excellent series of films. I recognised immediately that if transferred to the screen the Bond character would have universal appeal; men would want to be like him and women would fantasize about him. I felt that Fleming wrote about life in a new way, as a man of the world, and captured the vigour and excitement of life as he experienced it; combining his tastes for high living, exotic locations, sex, adventure – the good life.

I approached Ian Fleming's literary agent and discovered that the film rights had been optioned by Harry Saltzman. However he had been unable to interest anyone in the property, so we became partners and I took him to New York to meet Arthur Krim at United Artists. Shortly after that we began production on *Dr No*. Thus it was that one of the great heroes of the late twentieth-century cinema made his debut.

Ian Fleming was a great man, a great storyteller and great company. I enjoyed every moment that I spent with him and am glad that he lived to see the success of the first two films. He knew that the series would continue and I only wish he were alive today to see just how enduring his creation has been, I think he would have been very proud. Certainly I am proud to have been associated with James Bond and have had a wonderful time making the films with so many talented actors and technicians. If I had to pick one of the films as my favourite it would probably be *From Russia with Love*, as I feel it was with this film that the Bond formula and style were perfected.

The style of Bond has always been very important to me. Bond has always been a smartly dressed hero; he may not have been born into the British aristocracy, but for me (and many others) he epitomizes a certain inimitable British style, knowing what to wear, what to drink, what to say – and when to break the rules. Over the years each actor who

'Cubby' Broccoli,
Los Angeles, November 1965

has played him has brought something new to the Bond persona, enhanced different dimensions of the character of the world's most famous secret agent. Sean Connery captured the animal magnetism, danger and ironic humour of Bond; Roger Moore brought style, humour and a younger feel; Tim Dalton's Bond was gritty and tough; while Pierce Brosnan has looks, style and wit. Even George Lazenby, who only played Bond once, might have continued in the role if he had had a different attitude. (In a recent interview Lazenby said, "I didn't like the idea of playing Bond for the rest of my life, which, as it happens, I have been anyway…")

But whoever portrays him on the screen, James Bond will always have his followers: there will always be an audience for intriguing stories, dastardly villains and gorgeous girls. When we started to make the Bond films the Cold War was at its height – now the world is a very different place, but Bond himself has not really changed over the years. Regimes may rise and fall, lapels may widen or narrow, but there will always be villains to conquer and women to pursue. His methods may have changed to keep pace with the technology of the times, but ultimately he remains the old-fashioned, suited, hero.

Now....meet the most
extraordinary gentleman
spy in all fiction........
JAMES BOND
Agent 007...

007

THE FIRST JAMES BOND FILM ADVENTURE!

IAN FLEMING'S

Dr. No

007 THE DOUBLE "O" MEANS HE HAS
A LICENSE TO KILL WHEN HE CHOOSES...WHERE
HE CHOOSES...WHOM HE CHOOSES!

HARRY SALTZMAN and ALBERT R. BROCCOLI present IAN FLEMING'S Dr. No starring SEAN CONNERY as James Bond and URSULA ANDRESS JOSEPH WISEMAN JACK LORD also starring BERNARD LEE Screenplay by
RICHARD MAIBAUM, JOHANNA HARWOOD, and BERKLEY MATHER Directed by TERENCE YOUNG Music Composed by MONTY NORMAN Produced by HARRY SALTZMAN and ALBERT R. BROCCOLI EON PRODUCTIONS LTD. TECHNICOLOR® Released thru UNITED UA ARTISTS

Dr No, the sixth book
title in the series and
the first to be filmed,
opened in Britain in
1962 and May, 1963
in America. The poster
introduced the 007
trademark, guns, girls
and the remarkably
lasting concept of the
"gentleman spy"

HOW BOND
SAVED AMERICA - AND ME

Jay McInerney

*I*n the early months of 1963, the first American Pop Art exhibition opened at the Guggenheim, featuring among others Andy Warhol, Robert Rauschenberg and Jasper Johns; Medgar Evars, the Mississippi Civil Rights leader, was shot in the back and killed; and a Soviet woman, Valentina Tereshkova, orbited the Earth 45 times. The all-American crew cut was still fashionable in certain quarters, notably and regrettably within the realm ruled by my father. And in May of that uncertain year, the movie *Dr No* opened in New York. At the time it seemed to me that James Bond – along with John, Paul, George and Ringo, who arrived seconds later – had appeared, not a moment too soon, to save America, and not incidentally to liberate me from my crew cut and help me to meet girls.

I was only eight years old at the time and I was not allowed to go to the cinema to see *Dr No*. On hearsay, my parents judged it to be far too racy for me. There were kids at school whose parents were not so strict, and these lucky few told the rest of us exactly what we wanted to hear, and what our parents feared – that the movie was full of hot babes and cool weaponry. Not to mention Bond, James Bond, himself, who was reportedly everything we wanted to be. Barred from seeing the movie, I went undercover, quite literally: in some crafty manner – I can't remember the details now – I got hold of several of the original Ian Fleming novels and started reading them at night, under the sheets with a flashlight after I presumed my parents were in bed.

At the time James Bond slipped suavely into America, I was looking for a new role model after more than a year of worshipping Davy Crockett, as portrayed in the Disney movie by Fess Parker. Alongside Daniel Boone, Davy Crockett the rugged frontiersman had been the perfect hero for six- and seven-year-old American boys in the early Sixties. The whole point of Davy Crockett, right down to his nickname, was that he was uncultured, unpolished – a New World Rousseauvian Natural Man who wore animal skins and spoke the homespun unvarnished truth. He was what Americans call a straight shooter, both verbally and ballistically, someone who always tells the truth, and in Crockett's case happens to be able to knock a squirrel out of a tree at 300 yards. When in

Sean Connery, wearing a made-to-measure shirt, with unusual cuffs from Turnbull & Asser, fixes a Smirnoff 'vodkatini' while listening to music on the latest model Dansette record player, in this publicity shot for *Dr No*

(*Opposite*) In 1962, it was still important for some to dress for dinner, even if your clothes had come from *Dr No*'s oriental wardrobe. However terminal James Bond's situation appears to be, his neatly folded white pocket handkerchief gives a hint that all is not yet lost and that western culture will prevail

(*Top left*) The Fab Four in 1963. The velvet-collared and cuffed suits, double-breasted waistcoats and black knitted ties, echo "The Edwardian Look" of the 1950s

(*Top right*) The straight-shootin' Davy Crockett; Fess Parker in the Disney film of that name, raccoon-skin cap firmly and honestly in place

(*Right*) The feverish *Reefer Madness*, 1938, was still being screened in some high schools in the socially stiff America into which Bond was launched

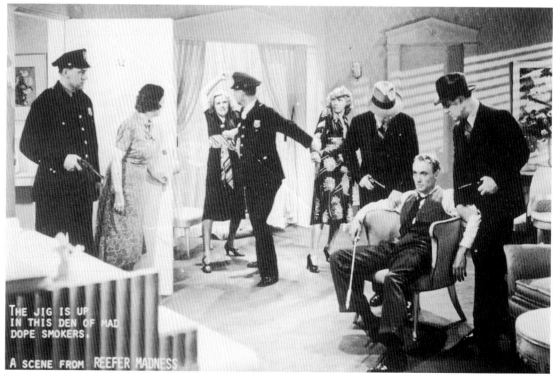

THE JIG IS UP IN THIS DEN OF MAD DOPE SMOKERS.

A SCENE FROM REEFER MADNESS

(*Left*) In *Dr No* James Bond saves the great American rocket launch. An *Apollo* spacecraft blasts off from Cape Canaveral

(*Below*) Yuri Gagarin and Valentina Tereshkova, Soviet cosmonauts who became the first man and the first woman in space, in 1961 and 1963 respectively

the movie, as in life, Crockett was elected to Congress from the state of Kentucky his rough manners and appearance, so amusing to the sophisticates of Washington D.C., vouchsafed his sincerity and honesty.

Like the ragtag American colonists who fought the impeccably tailored redcoats, Crockett stood for American authenticity against false (read "Old World") sophistication. But in the early Sixties, nearly 200 years after the Revolution, we seemed to have been secure enough to look back to the mother country for inspiration again. Or insecure enough – at that moment the Soviet Union appeared to be winning the space race, the Russkies having launched the first satellite, the first man in space and the first orbital mission. It is hardly insignificant that the final triumphant act of Bond in the film of *Dr No* is to save the great American rocket launch – phallic imagery, anyone? – from destruction by the eponymous villain. God, we needed Bond, all right.

Certainly I was ready. I believed it was time to put aside rustic and childish things – like raccoon-skin caps. To remember just how rugged and frontier-like American life was in many respects at that time, I recall that my family, living in a suburb near Seattle in 1963, had just discovered an exotic new food called pizza, and that aside from spaghetti, the only putatively European cuisine that made guest appearances on our dinner table was so-called French fries and so-called English muffins. Cheese was something

(*Left*) President Kennedy welcomes Soviet leader, Khrushchev to the American embassy in Vienna, June 3, 1961

(*Bottom left*) Cargo ship loaded with missiles under canvas, bound for Cuba in October 1962

(*Bottom right*) An aerial intelligence photograph shows Soviet missile sites in Cuba

(*Opposite*) Poster for the second Bond film, *From Russia with Love*, released in America in 1964

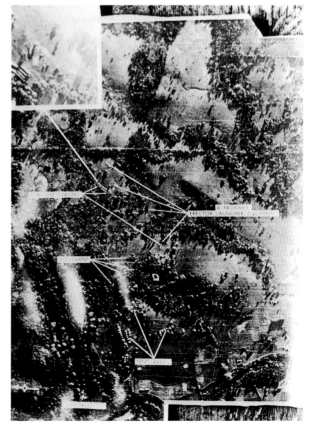

Meet James Bond, secret agent 007

His new incredible women...

His new incredible enemies...

His new incredible adventures...

HARRY SALTZMAN AND ALBERT R. BROCCOLI PRESENT

IAN FLEMING'S

FROM RUSSIA WITH LOVE

STARRING
SEAN CONNERY AS JAMES BOND

Also starring
PEDRO ARMENDARIZ   LOTTE LENYA
ROBERT SHAW   BERNARD LEE AS "M"

And
introducing   DANIELA BIANCHI

Screenplay by RICHARD MAIBAUM   Adapted by JOHANNA HARWOOD   Title Song Written by LIONEL BART   Orchestral Music Composed and Conducted by JOHN BARRY

Produced by HARRY SALTZMAN AND ALBERT R. BROCCOLI   Directed by TERENCE YOUNG

TECHNICOLOR®   EON PRODUCTIONS LTD. Released thru UNITED ARTISTS

orange that came packaged and pre-sliced from the supermarket, and it was called, appropriately enough, American cheese. Like the other men in our suburban neighbourhood, my dad wore a sack suit to work – that comfortable semi-shapeless American style which was supposed to equalize businessmen of many different physiques. Although I was unable to acquire Savile Row suits to replace my fringed buckskin jacket – didn't in fact know where or what Savile Row was – I knew when I finally saw them that Sean Connery's suit and tie looked a hell of a lot sharper than my dad's. And in the meantime, fuelled by the novels, I spent hours imagining myself as Bond, rescuing the girls I admired at school from Goldfinger and Dr No.

The country at large was undoubtedly ready for Bond. At that moment, when Sean Connery hit our shores in *Dr No*, we had a young president who had perhaps prepared us in many ways for the Bond invasion. In 1961, John Kennedy had listed *From Russia with Love* as one of his ten favourite novels in Life magazine, right after Stendhal's *The Red and the Black*, and it's easy to imagine the handsome young president identifying with the sophisticated secret agent. At the time we hardly knew just how much they had in common – those cynical and charming Cold Warriors and womanizers. But certainly Kennedy's endorsement had something to do with Bond's subsequent popularity on this

(*Opposite, far left*) Bond imitators came to the small screen in 1964. Robert Vaughn as Napoleon Solo in *The Man From U.N.C.L.E*

(*Opposite, left*) *Our Man Flint*, 1967. Their man, James Coburn, was one of the Bond imitators to have something of a style of his own

(*Right*) Some parents were seriously concerned about the morality of the bedroom scenes in all the early films, but they were crucial to the plots – and success – of the films. *From Russia with Love*, 1963

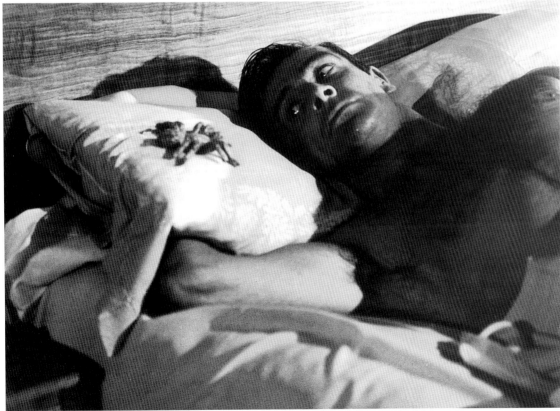

(*Left*) Bond rarely remained alone for long in any bedroom – here he contemplates what to do with an unwelcome visitor in *Dr No*

side of the world. Kennedy's example paved the way for the idea of the suave, manly hero in a trim two-button suit. Kennedy's adoption of the racy two-button over the three-button model was already proving tremendously influential to American business tailoring, just as his wife was influencing feminine fashion. Unlike most presidents and politicians, J. F. K. looked like a guy who could have stepped out of the pages of *Esquire* – and he slept with the girls who stepped out of the pages of *Playboy*, though we didn't know it at the time.

At the start of the decade the very concept of sophistication was still suspect. Urbanity was European, almost un-American. Anyone who knew too much about food and wine, or clothes, was suspected of – shall we say femininity? – and those men who were interested in such things had to look between the pages of pin-ups in men's magazines to find out, say, how to tie a Windsor knot, as if only in this securely heterosexual environment was it safe to discuss these matters. J. F. K., though, was clearly the kind of guy who would know how to tie a Windsor knot, and no one was going to question his masculinity. He was a war hero, and shortly before the Bond invasion of America he had faced down the Russians in the Cuban missile crisis. If the young president prepared us for Bond in some ways, the nationwide Kennedy cult which developed in the years following his assassination a few months after the opening of *Dr No* undoubtedly contributed to the further and continued appeal of 007. It must have given us some belated satisfaction that the dead president's British alter ego continued to elude assassins such as Rosa Klebb, Red Grant and Goldfinger.

Unfortunately, the year after J. F. K.'s assassination I was again forbidden from attending the new Bond movie, this one called *From Russia with Love*, which only served to increase my interest in all things Bondian. But Bondism was beginning to permeate the culture. That year, 1964, *The Man From U.N.C.L.E* hit the small screen; my best friend Mike Falcon and I were able to watch secret agent Napoleon Solo imitating Bond. It was followed within the year by *I-Spy* and *The Secret Agent*. The toy stores were full of Bond toys, and I continued my undercover reading of the novels. The whole concept of espionage appealed to my young mind in part, I think, because it fitted in with my notion of a secret identity, a secret Jay McInerney, fourth-grade student and nerd by day, glamorous womanizer who saves the world by night. From the moment that a boy first identifies the sexual impulse – which in my case was roughly 1963 – until the moment that he consummates his most profoundly burning ambition, life is a case of espionage.

Covert surveillance was a top priority – as when Nick Falcon and I hid inside a shower stall in the girls' locker room. The opposite sex was like Russia, in many senses.

The promotional
material for the
American release of
Goldfinger in 1965,
was guaranteed to
drive all teenagers
into hormonal
overdrive

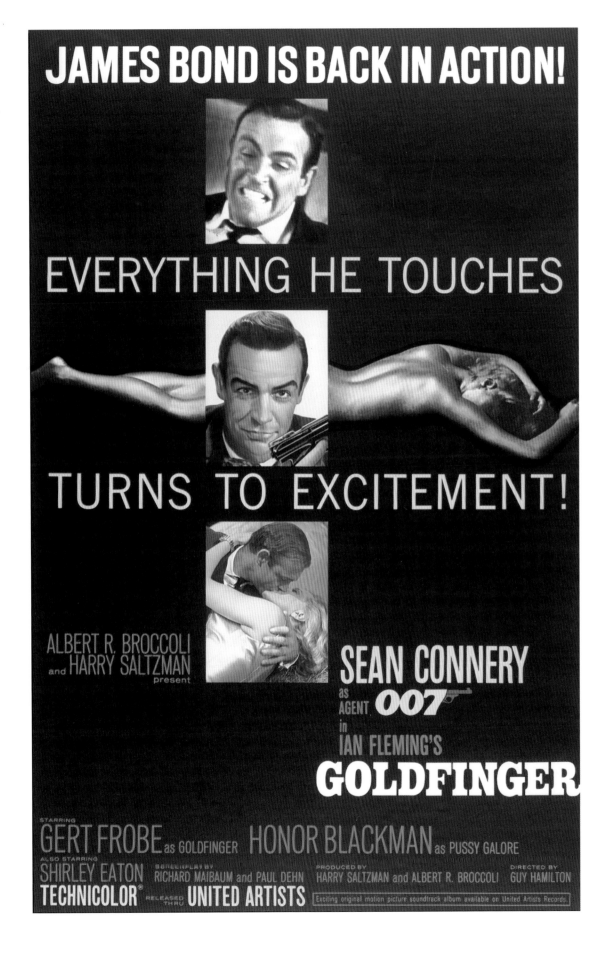

From the ages of about seven to 17 a boy's life becomes divided between his public and his top secret selves. "Undercover" becomes a concrete concept. And intrigue permeates one's daily existence. Mike Falcon and I paid a hood in our class, Richard Krebbs, some $20 for a pair of pointy-toed, stacked-heel, Italian-made "Beatle boots" which we hid in the woods on the way to school, knowing our parents would never let us wear them. Each morning, walking to the bus stop, we would duck into the woods and exchange our boring parent-approved shoes for the forbidden pointy boots – alternating this sartorial honour with each other – which were returned to their hiding place before we went home. Bond confirmed us in the knowledge of life as a secret mission.

In my reading of the novels I started with *Dr No*, and I was not disappointed; I recall it as being tremendously sexy, although looking back now it seems pretty tame stuff. Oddly, such being my perhaps dim grasp of the sexual question at the time, what I recall best is the scene in which the deadly centipede is released in Bond's bed and how it lingered in the area of his groin, this being, Ian Fleming reported, the warmest area of the male anatomy. This seemed like an exquisite and horrific detail to me, just the kind of thing to transfix an eight-year-old. Several years later, when I finally got to see the film, I was somewhat disappointed to see that a tarantula had been substituted for the centipede. Everyone knew tarantulas only looked scary – and it didn't even linger in the primary erogenous zone. But it was not Bond's body that I was interested in.

My secret night-time under-the-covers reading sessions were interrupted when my mother came across several of the Ian Fleming paperbacks underneath my bed. Her horrified reaction confirmed my sense of their sexiness. If my mother was that upset about them, they had to be good. When *Goldfinger* came out in '65, I was again forbidden to see it, though I was fully ten years old by this time, and in my own mind practically an adult. Between Beatles songs, Shirley Bassey's rendition of the *Goldfinger* song titillated me and my friends that summer, transistor radios pressed to our ears. Whether or not the films were actually restricted or whether it was a local cinema policy in Vancouver, where I was then living – or whether we simply imagined it – we were under the impression that we needed to be accompanied by an adult in order to get into the film.

Finally, when *Thunderball* was released, Mike Falcon and I could wait no longer. Our secret mission became this: to sneak into the cinema by any means possible. One Saturday we took our bikes downtown, hid them far from the cinema so as to look older than bike-riding age, and posted ourselves outside, furtively approaching any older men who looked remotely approachable, as we would later do outside of liquor stores, and asking them to pose as our fathers. Finally one of them said yes, took our money and

Jill Masterton (Shirley Eaton) dies a golden
death in *Goldfinger*, 1964

(*Top left*) The Bond films became an entertainment industry phenomenon, as acknowledged by this *Life* magazine cover

(*Top right*) The men's fashion industry also recognized the influence of the films. The April 1966 issue of American *GQ* featured Sean Connery in an editorial about the style of James Bond

(*Opposite*) The poster for *Thunderball*, 1965, which took the action underwater to great dramatic effect

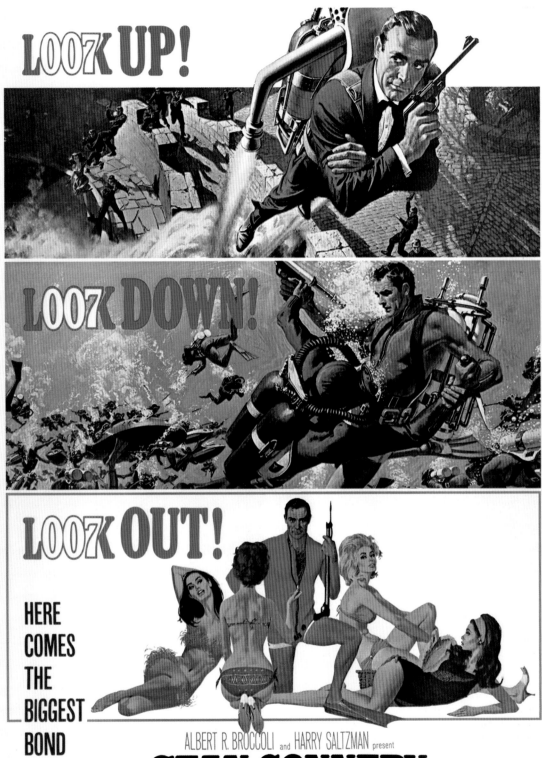

(*Left*) Largo briefs his men – an almost medieval expression of power

(*Below*) Sean Connery, oozing charm, hands Luciana Paluzzi "something to wear"; *Thunderball*, 1965

In the books, Ian Fleming used identifiable brands to more accurately define his hero, his opponents and the world in which they operated. The films adopted his technique – and sensing the added value to be gained – allowed chosen product partners to support the promotion of the films through their own advertising campaigns.

Sean Connery plays James Bond in the current release 'Dr. No'.

James Bond (and friend) await next assignment

Here he sits at the Dorchester bar, quietly nursing his Smirnoff in that lethal gun hand. At any minute a whisper from the barman, a telephone call from the indestructible M — and Bond will be off, his Walther PPK 7.65mm snug in its Berns Martin triple-draw holster. Destination? Anybody's guess.

Shooting today?

Let's be accurate. Actor Sean Connery (and friend Smirnoff) await next assignment—which, like as not, will be a hard day's work on the forthcoming Bond film. Connery was chosen for the lead because — well, because he fitted the part to perfection.

Connery's Smirnoff is in the best Bond tradition, too. So we asked if it was part of the 'getting-under-Bond's-skin' routine.

"No," he said, "I enjoyed Smirnoff long before I ever heard of Bond. Why? Well I know it's pretty popular these days — but that's not the reason. To me it's unique. Look at it. Clear as crystal. Pure — 100%. It leaves no trace on the breath, has the nicest after-effects, and goes wonderfully well with practically anything from tonic to orange juice. What am I drinking now? A Vodkatini."

He took 3 parts of Smirnoff, 1 part dry Vermouth, added ice, the essential lemon peel, and stirred well. He strained it, added another sliver of peel, and an olive. "Drink," he said.

We drank. It slipped down very nicely. Bond-Connery, perfectionist, smiled a connoisseur's smile.

SEAN CONNERY
The original James Bond

JIM BEAM
You can't improve on the original.

Two one-of-a-kind originals: SEAN CONNERY, the original and most famous James Bond. JIM BEAM, the world's finest Bourbon.

86 PROOF KENTUCKY STRAIGHT BOURBON WHISKEY. DISTILLED AND BOTTLED BY THE JAMES B. BEAM DISTILLING CO., CLERMONT, BEAM, KENTUCKY.

The Smirnoff 'advertorial' (*top left*) in the December 1962 issue of *Town Magazine* was so quick off the mark that it had to explain who the actor was playing: 'James Bond'

The Bond film formula which developed was to become a marketing man's dream – and 30 years on – still is. The clear, strong images created have been used both officially "under licence" and unofficially "by inference" as in these advertisements from the 60s and early 70s

motioned us to follow. And we were in. Never before or since have I felt so vividly the intimate promise of the cinema darkness in the moment after the lights go down. Beginning with the signature theme music and gun barrel opening, we were hooked.

James Bond on film was actually a far more appealing character than the guy in the books. As played to the hilt by Connery, he was less ruthless, more witty and polished than the original. We knew right away that he was everything we wanted to be. Two scenes seemed to me to sum up everything about this perfect role model, both involving the voluptuous Luciana Paluzzi, who vied in my later fantasies with the glorious Claudine Auger. In perhaps the most famous moment of the film, Connery surprises Paluzzi in his bathtub. When, after some suggestive banter, she asks Bond if he might hand her something to wear, he responds by holding out to her a pair of slippers. What confidence, what wit!

And then there was an exchange with super-villain Adolfo Celi at his oceanside mansion. Celi has been shooting skeet with Paluzzi. On Bond's arrival Paluzzi makes herself scarce, the better to prepare to kill Bond. But 007, with his trained eye, can tell that the automatic shotgun in Celi's hand is a slightly lighter weapon than standard. He tells Celi it looks like a woman's model. Celi says, "Ah, you know about guns, do you Mr Bond?" To which Connery replies, "Not really, but I know a little about women." I'm not sure that we actually stood up and applauded at this moment, but we might have. It was perhaps my first encounter with wry understatement, and I thoroughly approved.

Of course we loved the gadgets, which were just beginning to take prominence in the Bond films – the Aston Martin, the one-man jet pack, the mini subs – and we thought the underwater fight scenes were very cool, though it was the underwater love scene with Claudine Auger which intrigued us the most. Immediately after seeing the film I bought the single to the Tom Jones title song and played it till it wore out, alternating it on the turntable with "I Want To Hold Your Hand". At the time, the message of Bond, even more overtly than the message of The Beatles, was about sex.

As much as the Pill, Bond probably helped to usher in the sexual revolution. But it was also about style. Pre-Bond Americans weren't just puritanical about sex – they were also pragmatic, which is to say puritanical about style, about any triumph of form over function. Bond was urbanely cool: aside from being great-looking, as incarnated by Sean Connery, he was also witty and well-dressed and unflappable, the only movie hero we had ever seen whose first impulse, after killing a man, was to straighten his tie. And the message seemed to be that if you were stylish, women would want to sleep with you. Presumably it was something you could acquire with practice. I was too young to start

Man with a mission… *From Russia with Love*, 1963

JAY MCINERNEY

The films became a showplace for all the latest technology, both real and imagined. The first films were brilliantly packaged by Ken Adam, the production designer and his skilled team at Pinewood Studios, just outside London. (*Opposite*) Ken Adam's design for the SPECTRE base hidden in the crater in *You Only Live Twice*, 1967 and the film version

(*Right and below*) Losing all sense of gravity... *Moonraker* sets, 1979

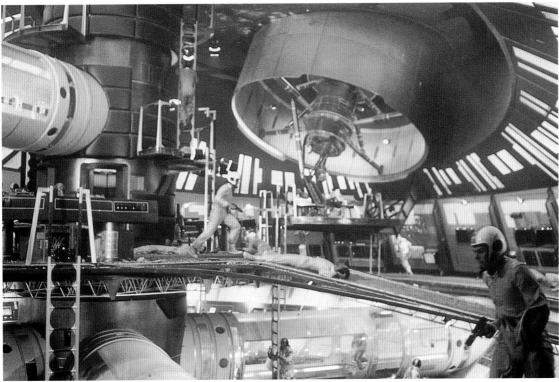

drinking vodka martinis or Dom Perignon '55, and likewise too young to imitate the shirts, ties and particularly the suits so sleekly tailored by Anthony Sinclair in London. The budget for a whole collection of suits for Connery to wear in *From Russia with Love* was reportedly a then-impressive £1,000, which is half the price of a single bespoke suit in Savile Row, now. But as a kid somewhat small for my age, I was pleased with the idea that thuggish physicality didn't necessarily count for everything with girls.

Connery's Bond provided a kind of role model that hadn't existed in the US before then – a cultured man who knew how to navigate a wine list, how to field-strip a Beretta, and how to seduce women. He was like the *Playboy* "Advisor" – that faceless feature of our favourite magazine, the man who knew how to do everything, who knew what to wear and what to say in any situation. With the exception of William Powell in the *Thin Man* series, American male role models had tended toward the strong, silent type: the taciturn and slightly scruffy detective as epitomized by Bogart's Sam Spade, and the cowboy gunslinger à la John Wayne. It is difficult to overestimate the influence of the Bond films, which probably had as great an impact on the culture as anything since Elvis, generating from the beginning a slew of imitations, including the James Coburn's *Our Man Flint* (1966) and *In Like Flint* (1967) as well as Lindsay Shonteff's *Licence To Kill* and a dozen others up to *True Lies* (1994).

Connery was probably the first movie hero to cap a killing with a quip, a tradition which continued through the *Indiana Jones* and *Die Hard* movies. Although George Lucas deliberately conceived of Indiana Jones, *contra* Bond, as a rough-and-tumble character with only one set of clothes and a beat-up hat, the series owes much, including the hero's tongue-in-cheek wit, to Bond, a debt which Lucas acknowledged when he cast Connery as Jones's father. In the *Die Hard* films it is of course the villains who dress in well-cut suits and speak in European accents: detective John McClane's filthy ripped T-shirts seem intended to vouch for his all-American authenticity. Personally I'm getting tired of ripped T-shirts, and I am relieved that Pierce Brosnan has revived the well-tailored suit.

It is a very different world that Bond comes to save in the mid-Nineties, and there was a fear that the children of the moment would see Bond as a sex-addicted, alcoholic murderer. On the other hand, viewing the old classic Bond movies they might recognize the visual style and music of the early Sixties which have enjoyed a revival recently. 1995 saw the revival of the narrow-legged, skinny-lapel suit, solid ties and even Carnaby Street-style velvet for men, as well as the bright coloured shift for women. Bands like Deee-Lite and Portishead are reviving the sound of the time: indeed Portishead had a big underground hit with a song that is eerily reminiscent of Monty Norman's distinctive Bond theme – though it in fact samples the *Man From U.N.C.L.E.* theme.

And it has to be said that the fashions and visual style of the early Bond era – as well as Ken Adam's wonderful futuristic sets – look far more classic and enduringly appealing than the contemporary style of the late Sixties and Seventies which appears in the later Bond movies. Roger Moore, stylish and cosmopolitan though he may be, does now look a little silly in his wide lapels and flared trousers. Connery's wardrobe in the first four films, shot between '62 and '65, would look perfect in almost any setting in 1995: the trim two-button suit in grey and blue with side vents, the white or light blue shirt with spread collar and the black silk knit tie. At this date it is safe to say that the styles of the early to mid-Sixties have an air of classicism about them, particularly when contrasted with the baroque, post-*Sergeant Pepper* aesthetic of the later part of the decade and the rococo excesses of the Seventies. Pure Sixties though it is, as crystallized in the early Connery films, Bond style is beginning to appear timeless. And every day, millions of men who grew up in the Sixties look in the mirror in the hope of seeing something Bondian there, and thousands more say something to a woman which they imagine to be Bondian, whether they are conscious of it or not.

Not long ago my wife watched patiently as I was measured for my first bespoke suit at Huntsman, in Savile Row. The night before, I had subjected her to a wine-tasting with some of my British friends. When I was finished with my fitting she asked, "Wherever did you get this interest in clothes and wine and food?" What she meant was, this excessive interest. She knew that only one of the above held any interest for my father, and she was curious. At the time I didn't have an answer. But now I know. I guess I would have to say that it comes from Bond. James Bond.

THE WORLD OF 007

Nick Foulkes

To get the most out of the novels of Ian Fleming it is perhaps best to read them almost as if they were historical works rather than adventure fiction. Read them much as you would a novel by Trollope, to gain through the working out of the plot an insight into the obsessions and preoccupations, the habits of dress and behaviour of the day. Just as the reader of Trollope is intrigued to see how the dashing Phineas Finn, the lady-killing Irish MP of the Palliser novels, will fare in the turbulent world of Victorian politics, so the reader of a Fleming novel wishes to know what will become of the dashing James Bond, the lady-killing spy, in his turbulent world, that of Cold War espionage.

Further comparisons can be drawn: Trollope for example liked to include fox-hunting passages in his books, in the same way as Fleming had gambling scenes of one kind or another appear in many of his; both writers have enjoyed the accolades of the leaders of western powers (John Major is a famous Trollope fan; and John Kennedy loved the Bond books) and both enjoyed huge commercial success during their lifetimes. But whereas Trollope depicted British life during the greatest period of prestige this country has ever known, Fleming's novels depict a nation rapidly forgetting how to be great.

Postwar Britain, although at peace after six years of conflict, still endured the privations of war, including rationing – and a price limit on meals in cafés and restaurants continued to be enforced until 1950. In 1946 a strike crippled London's smart hotels and restaurants. On one day Simpsons-in-the-Strand was reduced to serving only cold chicken, and on another day the Ritz was unable to serve lunch at all, except to a few special customers. Once the Labour government of Clement Attlee had nationalized coal and most of the other major industries, a new order began to emerge; in 1947 Sir Ben Smith, chairman of the West Midlands division of the Coal Board, announced that Himley Hall, historic seat of the Earls of Dudley, was to serve as a regional HQ. To cap it all the weather was atrocious, the winter of 1946-47 being one of the harshest in living memory, and made worse by choking fogs which covered London buildings in grey smut.

Many must have felt like Major Dexter Smythe, the protagonist of Fleming's novella *Octopussy*, who decided to flee to Jamaica with his horde of Nazi gold and his charming middle-class wife Mary, a former Wren. "He got passages for them both in one of the early banana boats sailing from Avonmouth to Kingston, Jamaica, which they both agreed would be a paradise of sunshine, good food and cheap drink and a glorious haven from the gloom, restrictions and Labour government of post-war England."

In a way Major Dexter Smythe OBE, Royal Marines (Retd) can be seen as a metaphor for the post-war England into which Bond was born. He is described as "the remains of a once brave and resourceful officer and of a handsome man." Now, aged 54, he is going bald, has a sagging belly, has suffered two coronary thromboses, drinks too heavily and is gnawed by the inner canker of an ancient crime. Nevertheless, "in his well-chosen clothes, his varicose veins out of sight and his stomach flattened by a discreet support belt behind an immaculate cummerbund, he was still a fine figure of a man at a cocktail party or dinner."

Taking Major Smythe as emblematic of post-war Britain, it is not difficult to read a certain authorial distaste for a slothful nation that has gone soft after the war, complacent about its position in the world: a nation attempting to punch above its weight. In *You Only Live Twice*, Bond's Japanese counterpart Tiger Tanaka's deliberately provocative outburst brands Britain as "the pitiful ruins of a once great power", happy to wallow in nostalgic gossip about aristocrats and royalty while the country is run by indolent trade unionists. But it is a picture which elicits the required spirited response from a riled Bond.

As Anthony Burgess once pointed out, "when *Casino Royale* appeared in 1953, it had a message for the British people. Tough, brave and yet no cold-bath ascetic, Bond reminded his readers of qualities they seemed to have lost. Eight years after the end of World War II, the age of the great heroes who had built and sustained an empire was long over. Now instead we had the bickerings and intrigues of the superpowers. The situation was humiliating."

Yet despite the new world order, by the terms of which Britain was essentially a spectator, the old world order seemed still to apply in England, superficially at least. By 1951 Winston Churchill was again prime minister, a man who had taken part in the last cavalry charge ever undertaken by the British army. The country his Conservative administration governed was entering a new Elizabethan age; a beautiful young queen was crowned in 1952 and later in the year she walked up 50 yards of red carpet, boarded an aircraft and began a tour of her empire, with an entourage of some 30 staff.

"Well-run, well staffed and with the finest cuisine and cellar in the Caribbean" is how Ian Fleming described the Queen's Club, in Kingston, Jamaica. The British agent, Strangways leaves the club for the last time, at the beginning of *Dr No*, 1962

A couple en route to Royal Ascot, observed
by two soldiers and Henri Cartier-Bresson,
Waterloo station, 1953

However it was also during the 1950s that the process of decolonization, started during the Labour administration, speeded up. Its ramifications were not lost on Ian Fleming, as is evident in the opening chapter of his 1958 novel *Dr No*, when he describes No 1 Richmond Road, Kingston, Jamaica:

"From the road a gravel path leads up to the pillared entrance through wide lawns marked out with tennis courts on which this evening, as on all evenings, the sprinklers are at work. This mansion is the social Mecca of Kingston. It is Queen's Club, which, for 50 years, has boasted the power and frequency of its blackballs.

"Such stubborn retreats will not long survive in modern Jamaica. One day Queen's Club will have its windows smashed and perhaps be burned to the ground, but for the time being it is a useful place to find in a subtropical island – well-run, well-staffed and with the finest cuisine and cellar in the Caribbean."

Bond may battle it out on the world stage, but the effect of the changing world order is sometimes seen in a more human perspective. In *For Your Eyes Only*, it is the uncertainty over Batista's crumbling regime in Cuba which causes the odious Major Gonzales and his two henchmen, "both carrying that new holdall of the tropics – a Pan American overnight bag," to gun down the Havelocks, after they refuse to sell Content, the 20,000-acre Jamaican plantation "given to an early Havelock by Oliver Cromwell as a reward for having been one of the signatories to King Charles's death warrant." The Havelock family "had maintained the plantation through three centuries, through earthquakes and hurricanes and through the boom and bust of cocoa, sugar, citrus and copra," only to become victims of the new world order.

It was into this changing world with its shifting values that James Bond was launched. Bond is part reactionary and part rebel. He belongs both to the world as it was before World War II and to the world of the Cold War and the Iron Curtain. World War II is constantly referred to throughout the novels and is the period during which, one suspects, the majority of Bond's world-view was formed. He needs to be old enough to have fought in the war, but still young enough not to ponder too much as he begins to at the start of *Live and Let Die*:

"The state of your health, the state of the weather, the wonders of nature – these are things that rarely occupy the average man's mind until he reaches the middle thirties. It is only on the threshold of middle age that you don't take them all for granted, just part of an unremarkable background to more urgent, more interesting things."

The desired fusion in Bond of a man with the harrowing experience of war (which enables him when invited to sample the smell of death by Scaramanga in *The Man with*

The young Queen Elizabeth II with the
Duke of Edinburgh, at the Coronation
Review of the Royal Air Force, July 1953

the Golden Gun to reply, "Thanks. I've tried it. I recommend the Berlin vintage, 1945… But I expect you were too young to be at that tasting") with the youthful impetuosity of a man who is willing to keep himself in top physical shape and keep on risking his life, results in an interesting problem: the age of 007. He is the Peter Pan of espionage, seemingly no older whether the prime minister is Churchill or Macmillan, the president Eisenhower or Kennedy or the Soviet leader Stalin or Khrushchev.

In *Casino Royale* James Bond is said to have bought his Amherst Villiers supercharged $4\frac{1}{2}$-litre Bentley in 1933. Yet by the time M writes his obituary for *The Times*, after Bond goes missing and is presumed dead in *You Only Live Twice*, Bond is said to have been 17 years old in 1941, meaning that he would have been about nine when he bought his first Bentley: a little precocious even by the standards of 007. But in the fantastic world of James Bond it is best to employ a little willing suspension of disbelief. He will always be more or less as he is described in *Moonraker*, "the rather saturnine young man in his middle thirties… Something a bit cold and dangerous in that face. Looks pretty fit. May have been attached to Templer in Malaya. Or Nairobi. Mau Mau work. Tough-looking customer."

Cold, dangerous, fit, tough, the adjective "versatile" might also have been added. Bond is a man who flits between the jazz and strip clubs of Harlem and the all-male clubs of St James's. He may be reactionary and sexist but he is a rebel as well, a man that despises those who, like the Old Wykehamist secret agent in *Living Daylights*, do things by the book. He is patriotic and reveres the old world order, yet is impatient with the old buffers who get in his way, such as Griffon Or Pursuivant, the eccentric herald at the College of Arms in *On Her Majesty's Secret Service*, who tries in vain to convince him of possible connections with an extinct baronetcy.

Fleming, in his fiction at least, seems to have had little time for social snobs. Like William Douglas-Home in his play *The Reluctant Debutante*, Fleming casts a jaundiced eye over the brittle world of English debs in the opening chapters of *The Spy Who Loved Me*, while in *On Her Majesty's Secret Service* it is Blofeld's desire to secure a title which leads Bond to him. And, significantly, when Bond is offered a title on his own merits in *The Man with the Golden Gun*, he refuses – about the only politically correct gesture he ever makes.

A character of contrasts, Bond was perfectly poised to explore what Andrew Lycett, in his excellent biography of Ian Fleming, calls the "disturbing moral ambiguity of a post-war world that could produce traitors like Burgess and Maclean." Lycett says of the Bond character in *Casino Royale* that although he is presented like "Bulldog Drummond

with all the trappings of a traditional British fictional secret agent, such as his Bentley, in fact he needs 'Marshall Aid' from Leiter to enable him to continue his baccarat game with Le Chiffre, the villain. Bond is rescued from his kidnapper not by the British or the Americans but by the Russians, who complete the job he should have done of eliminating Le Chiffre."

At other times, Bond is simply fighting World War II all over again. Wherever possible in his books Fleming works in some piece of anti-German rhetoric. In *The Hildebrand Rarity*, Krest the apparent American is revealed to have German, worse, Prussian ancestry: "So that was it! The old Hun again. Always at your feet or at your throat… what must this woman have to put up with, this beautiful girl he had got hold of to be his slave – his English slave?"

In *Moonraker*, in many ways one of the best Bond books and one which bears virtually no relation to the film of the same name, Sir Hugo Drax, the villain, not only cheats at cards, but turns out to be a German aristocrat and fervent Nazi who intends to destroy London with a nuclear rocket, which is little more than an updated V2. Drax drives a new Mercedes, Bond of course his Bentley. The Russians are only bit players whose function is to provide Drax with technical support and a means of escape – and to be identified in Fleming's demonology with the evils of Nazi Germany.

It may indeed be a confusing world, but you can usually rely on a German to be up to no good, and any other confusing feelings Bond might have tend to be dealt with by his boss M, who orders him to do what must be done and upon whom the morality, if there is any, of Bond's actions is devolved, thus effectively absolving Bond of anything but the most cursory feelings of anxiety. Bond may occasionally be assaulted by Hamlet-like qualms about his job; his oh-so-English scruples about shooting an apparently unarmed man almost cost him his life in *The Man with the Golden Gun*; but not M. Nothing seems to bother him, sitting in his club in a dark grey suit and bow tie knotted with Churchillian looseness: "It was difficult to believe that an hour before he had been playing with a thousand live chessmen against the enemies of England: that there might

(*Left*) Colonel-General Ivan Serov, chief of the Soviet secret police, arrives in London aboard a Tu-104 – the first Soviet jet airliner – in April 1956, to make arrangements for the visit of Khrushchev and Bulganin

(*Bottom*) The Berlin Wall, erected in 1961, set in concrete Churchill's concept of the Iron Curtain, which had divided Europe for the previous 15 years

BRITISH NAVAL COMMANDER MURDERED

In the early hours of this morning, in an Hong Kong Hotel bedroom, was discovered the body of the British Naval Commander James Bond.

The body was discovered by two Police Inspectors of the Hong Kong Police Force, who answered an emergency call from a nearby bar. The gunfire was heard by people in the street below, and the police were on the scene within minutes.

As yet there has been no arrest made, but the police are working on a definite clue. Foul play is suspected and the question is being asked what a high ranking naval officer was doing in such a notorious district.

(*Left*) The newspaper report of the murder which M staged so that Bond could go into deep cover in *You Only Live Twice*

(*Below*) Guy Burgess, the Foreign Office official who had been spying for Russia, defected in June 1951 and died there in obscurity in 1963

(*Left*) The Cambridge-educated Donald Maclean, the other Foreign Office official who disappeared with Burgess. The possibility of the continued existence of a third undiscovered traitor overshadowed the relationship between British and American Secret Services for over ten years

(*Left*) Young men in white tie and tails attend Queen Charlotte's Ball for debutantes, London, *c.* 1952

(*Opposite*) Jiving at The Savoy Ballroom, Harlem, New York, in the Fifties; James Bond as Fleming saw him would have felt as much at home there as at the Savoy Hotel in London

be, this evening, fresh blood on his hands, or a successful burglary, or the hideous knowledge of a disgusting blackmail case."

According to Andrew Lycett, M was based on Admiral Godfrey; it could also be said however, that there is more than a little of Churchill about him, and this extends beyond a shared taste in spotted bow ties. There is a ruthlessness about M, just as there was about Churchill.

As well as being the protector of the world that Bond is sent out to defend, M is also a symptom of it. The Victorian upbringing alluded to in *From Russia with Love* seems to be responsible for many of his views. For instance, in *Moonraker* his primary concern is that Hugo Drax's cheating at cards may result in a scandal along the lines of the Tranby Croft affair. But as well as allowing a suitably Victorian outlet for his fears, *Moonraker* also shows Fleming at his most lyrical about life in England. Fleming was a devotee

The clubs of Pall Mall and St James figure prominently in the world of Whitehall, and provided the model for Fleming's Blades. The dining room of Boodles will have witnessed many an intrigue over the celery and stilton

Fleming's Bond was at ease at gaming tables anywhere in
the world: Sean Connery, Claudine Auger and Adolfo Celi
as Bond, Domino and Largo, *Thunderball*, 1965

of clubland and a member of White's as well as the memorable Boodle's. His fondness for this kind of life is well expressed in his description of the "beautiful white and gold Regency dining room at Blades", described as "the most exclusive club in London" and, in short, the perfect place to consume pre-war Wolfschmidt, Mouton Rothschild '34 and Dom Perignon '46.

"It was a sparkling scene. There were perhaps 50 men in the room, the majority in their dinner jackets, all at ease with themselves and their surroundings, all stimulated by the peerless food and drink, all animated by a common interest – the prospect of high gambling, the grand slam, the ace pot, the key-throw in a 64 game at backgammon. There might be cheats or possible cheats amongst them, men who beat their wives, men with perverse instincts, greedy men, cowardly men, lying men; but the elegance of the room invested each one with a kind of aristocracy.

"At the far end, above the cold table, laden with lobsters, pies, joints and delicacies in aspic, Romney's unfinished full-length portrait of Mrs Fitzherbert gazed provocatively across at Fragonard's *Jeu de Cartes*, the broad conversation-piece which half-filled the opposite wall above the Adam fireplace. Along the lateral walls, in the centre of each gilt-edged panel, was one of the rare engravings of the Hell-Fire Club, in which each figure is shown making a minute gesture of scatological or magical significance."

Fleming wants the reader, like Bond, to drink in the "warm elegance of the scene". The world is meticulously created down to the idiosyncrasies of club life; when giving change, Blades pays out brand new notes and change, much in the same way that Boodle's will bring the bill with the correct change already on the salver. It is almost as if he is saying that the values of St James's are the values for which men have fought and died over the centuries, and that they are still worth fighting and dying for today – listen hard and it is almost possible to hear the strains of "Land of Hope and Glory".

Later in the same book there is a similarly lyrical passage: Bond and Gala stopped "for a moment on the edge of the great chalk cliff and stood gazing over the whole corner of England where Caesar had first landed 2,000 years before." Even at the height of a car chase when a car radio is switched on and the prime minister's voice is heard, Gala reflects that his is "the voice of all the great occasions in her life".

Yet Churchill, Blades, Buckingham Palace, the "nursemaids in the park, the birds in the trees", perhaps even the very countryside surveyed by Caesar 2,000 years ago will be destroyed if Drax has his dastardly way. Which of course in the end he does not.

But to present the world celebrated by Fleming and defended by Bond as merely Blimpish, xenophobic, unchanging and smugly Victorian would be wrong. The changes

The model for M? Sir Winston Churchill in the Cabinet Room at 10 Downing Street, on his 79th birthday, November 30, 1953

M was played by Bernard Lee in the first 11 films; he is seen here in his last one, *Moonraker*, 1979

of the time are constantly making themselves felt through the books. As the heads of the various American security organizations change their names are duly noted and commented on. The passing of the old-fashioned £5 note is mourned in *Goldfinger*. The metamorphosis of a Berlin bombsite into Checkpoint Charlie is mentioned in *The Living Daylights*. Even the introduction of such things as one-way traffic systems in London are faithfully recorded. When directing Bond to an auction at Sotheby's in *The Property of a Lady*, Mr Snowman of the jeweller Wartski's is careful to say, "It's not the old Georgian entrance in Bond Street... They have an awning and a red carpet out from their back door now that Bond Street's one-way."

The novels also point up various idiosyncrasies of the time; there is for example the ambivalent attitude towards drugs. In *Casino Royale* Bond takes a disapproving, almost risibly lofty stance towards narcotics, describing Le Chiffre's use of a Benzedrine inhaler as an offensive pantomime and analysing the addiction of one of his henchmen. "Bond guessed that he would kill without interest or concern for what he killed and that he would prefer strangling. He had something of Lennie in *Of Mice and Men*, but his

Traditional uniformed nannies perambulating their
charges, Kensington Gardens, London, 1960

inhumanity would not come from infantilism but from drugs. Marihuana, decided Bond." Etymology notwithstanding, the effectiveness of a stoned assassin remains somewhat open to speculation.

Yet Bond from time to time takes Benzedrine to sharpen his awareness, as did Fleming himself. In *Moonraker* there is even one occasion, certainly no less theatrical than that involving Le Chiffre, when a page delivers the drug to Bond at dinner, whereupon he unapologetically shovels half an envelope of the stuff into his Dom Perignon, which he then stirs with a scrap of toast just to make sure it is properly mixed. Nor is heroin universally reviled: at the beginning of *Goldfinger* Bond has just been clearing up some messy business to do with opium poppies. "In England, the Government, urged on by the United Nations' drive against drug-smuggling, announced that heroin would be banned in Britain. There was alarm in Soho and also among respectable doctors who wanted to save their patients agony. Prohibition is the trigger of crime."

The implied parallel is surely with the outlawing of alcohol in America in the Twenties. The man who arranges the smuggling is "a pleasant-spoken Import and Export merchant called Blackwell", who "decided that if he could make a fortune and at the same time help suffering humanity he had found the Secret of Life." It is only the actions of a "bad man" in England, who dilutes the heroin in Pimlico and sells it to "teddy boys" in dance halls and amusement arcades, which is overtly condemned.

It seems therefore acceptable to take drugs with Dom Perignon in smart surroundings but not in front of a pinball machine in a late-night coffee bar. Drugs were an acceptable tool to make one more alert or to put one to sleep and perhaps even tolerated as a smart person's indulgence, so long as they were procured from a Harley Street doctor or under the counter from some smart quasi-Victorian chemist in St James's. They only became unacceptable when bought by a teddy boy with a flick knife in the lavatory of a suburban dance hall.

This is of course an extreme picture but the battle against drugs is only hinted at in *Goldfinger* and forms the basis of just one short story, called *Risico*. It was only in the early Seventies, after Fleming's death, that attitudes changed enough to allow *Live and Let Die*, originally written as a Rider Haggardesque yarn about voodoo and pirates' gold, to be reworked as a blaxploitation movie about heroin trafficking.

Although Bond may not have altered much during the years that the novels were published, the world did. The affluence of the British population grew and the Conservatives were able to win the 1959 general election largely on the strength of what would now be called the feel-good factor. This was the climate of general prosperity which allowed

Air travel in the early days was a glamourous business, a world away from today's often packed departure-lounges. Stewardesses were picked for their looks first and passengers were letting the side down if not smartly dressed

(*Opposite*) Ian Fleming was an early air-travel enthusiast, writing both details of the flights and their destinations into his stories

(*Left*) Princess Elizabeth arrives in Montreal with the Duke of Edinburgh, in 1951, to begin a 10,000 mile tour of Canada, mainly by air

(*Below*) The newly opened airport at Salisbury, Rhodesia, with a Lockheed Constellation on the apron, prepares for a visit by the Queen Mother, July 1957

(*Left*) A Pan American Stratocruiser. These planes flew the London Heathrow–New York Idlewild Atlantic route in the 1950s

(*Opposite*) The Bond films introduced cinema audiences to the idea of long distance travel and being able to visit exotic locations, years before it became a possibility for all but a fortunate few: a chart of the locations used in the making of *The Spy Who Loved Me*, 1977

007

WORLD-WIDE LOCATIONS
FOR

"THE SPY WHO LOVED ME"

Harold Macmillan famously to proclaim, "You've never had it so good." And as the horizons of the British public broadened, so did Bond's. In *Casino Royale* a jaunt across the Channel to an old-fashioned northern French resort is deemed sufficiently exotic, but Bond quickly acquires a taste for foreign travel, and always succeeds in keeping one step ahead of the majority of his readers, dashing off to sundry European locations, America, the Caribbean, Canada, the Indian Ocean and in the penultimate novel, *You Only Live Twice*, Japan.

He is also perpetually curious about innovations. Everyday life in America is full of such fascinations for him and there is often a remark about the quality of central heating or the efficacy of air-conditioning. *The Spy Who Loved Me* contains a whole essay on the fixtures and fittings of the American motel of the early Sixties. Similarly, when faced with the technical wizardry employed by his opponents, be it the cunningly disguised forest hideout in *A View to a Kill*, the ingenuity of Dr No's underwater library or the sheer sleek killing power of Drax's rocket, Bond is full of rapt admiration.

Although he may have a Victorian boss, Bond is very much a creature of the second half of the twentieth century.

Predictably then, it is not just the destinations which excite Bond, but the ways of getting there. Fleming takes a joy in describing long-distance travel in meticulous detail – there is clear relish at the thought of the flight across the Atlantic in *Diamonds Are Forever.*

"The aircraft trembled against its brakes as the captain revved the four engines, one at a time, up to take-off speed, and through his window Bond watched the wing flaps being tested. Then the great plane turned slowly towards the setting sun, there was a jerk as the brakes were released and the grass on the other side of the runway flattened as, gathering speed, the Monarch hurtled down the two miles of stressed concrete and rose into the west, aiming ultimately for another little strip of concrete carpet on the other side of the world."

Bond delights in every aspect of the flight, the stop at Shannon airport, the sight of the gaudy gimcracks and gewgaws at the tawdry airport shop, the goblet of Irish Coffee – then a new and exotic drink far removed from today's steakhouse staple – before returning to the air to experience that "moment of exhilaration as the sun came up over the rim of the world and bathed the cabin in blood" and eat the BOAC "English country house breakfast" 20,000 feet above Nova Scotia.

Yes, for two shillings and sixpence the suburban commuter taking a Tube train to work was certainly transported, to a world blessedly far removed from the dreary reality of rented rooms in Peckham, a drab office in the City and a frugal lunch purchased with carefully hoarded Luncheon Vouchers. And a Bond novel was also just the sort of book with which the insomniac international traveller might choose to while away the few hours between a steak and champagne supper and a BOAC breakfast. In *On Her Majesty's Secret Service*, at Blofeld's ski resort the Piz Gloria, the reader is even introduced by name to various members of the "international set", including Lady Daphne Straight, an old girlfriend of Fleming's, Sir George Dunbar, an old friend of Fleming's, and Ursula Andress, who of course became the first Bond girl in the film version of *Dr No*. Indeed the game of spotting Fleming's friends and acquaintances can be played with many of his books. The name Michael "Shady" Tree, given to an American gangster in *Diamonds Are Forever*, is borrowed from the society painter Michael Tree, while the alias David Somerset used by Bond in *From Russia with Love* was the name of the present Duke of Beaufort.

And when, like any self-respecting member of the "international set", Bond sauntered down the steps of the double-decker Stratocruiser, he would be faced with some exotic sight, a beautiful girl, and something good to eat; take the breakfast he enjoys on arrival in Kingston, Jamaica in *Live and Let Die.*

"Paw-paw with a slice of green lime, a dish piled with red bananas, purple star-apples and tangerines, scrambled eggs and bacon, Blue Mountain coffee – the most delicious in the world – Jamaican marmalade, almost black, and guava jelly."

"As Bond, wearing shorts and sandals, had his breakfast on the veranda and gazed down on the sunlit panorama of Kingston and Port Royal, he thought how lucky he was and what wonderful moments of consolation there were for the darkness and danger of his profession."

In his writing Fleming had an enormous appetite for these physical moments of "consolation", be it a pot of Blue Mountain coffee, the feel of a perfectly balanced firearm nestling in a shoulder holster, the contented bubbling of those famous twin exhausts, a tastefully decorated room, a bottle of Mr Trumper's Eucris, a cake of Floris soap, the dry riffle of cards in a casino late at night, a morning spent scuba-diving off some exotic coral reef, or of course those seemingly endless, faultless, pairs of beautiful firm breasts.

To borrow Alan Bates's opening lines from the mid-Sixties film *Nothing But the Best:* "Face it, it's a filthy stinking world, but there are some smashing things in it."

British Army officers, on secondment to Whitehall, wearing "mufti" – dark tailored suits, white shirts, striped ties, bowler hats and umbrellas – in Hyde Park in the Fifties

THE STYLE SECRETS
OF JAMES BOND

Nick Foulkes

*T*here are moments of great luxury in the life of a secret agent." As first sentences of novels go, this one, from *Live and Let Die*, has almost the same ring of self-confident, self-evident, unassailable veracity to it as Jane Austen's famous "It is a truth universally acknowledged, that a single man in possession of a good fortune, must be in want of a wife." Luxury, a sense of style and the life of a secret agent were quite insep-arable in the mind of Bond's creator Ian Fleming – and even by the luxurious standards of secret agents, James Bond gets a good slice: there can have been very few people who, in 1953, the year *Casino Royale* was published, encountered the same kind of difficulties as James Bond. "The trouble always is," he explains to Vesper, "not how to get enough caviar, but how to get enough toast with it."

But secret agents, even the fictional 007, have to at least maintain a veneer of se-crecy, a certain modesty of appearance which should not seem out of place anywhere in the world. Besides, in the world of cold showers, racing changes, firearms training and unarmed combat, a dandified appearance or an excessive attention to matters sartorial would be distinctly inappropriate. Those "calm, grey, damnably clear eyes" of M's would either spring from their sockets in surprise or else avert themselves in distaste if Bond were to sit across his large central desk, in his green-carpeted office on the eighth floor of that building near Regent's Park, and start adjusting the knot in a florid silk tie or toying with a pair of diamond and pink enamel cuff links. No, it is left to the likes of "Pistols" Scaramanga from *The Man with the Golden Gun* to wear the co-respondent shoes and have a high white silk stock secured by "a gold pin in the shape of a miniature pistol", or Blofeld in *You Only Live Twice* to parade around in Oriental armour, including a spiked and winged helmet, or a black silk kimono decorated with a golden dragon.

Bond's uniform – and it almost is a uniform, so little does it vary in the course of the books – is simple. Indeed in the last Bond novel, *The Man with the Golden Gun*, the "dark-blue single-breasted suit, white shirt, thin black knitted silk tie, black casuals" are referred to even by a Major Townsend, an operative in an obscure branch of the service, as 007's "usual rig". Bond's taste in suits has by then become so much of an open secret

that it is known even to the Soviets (shades of Oleg Gordievsky, who recently revealed that in real life the Bond films were required viewing for KGB agents). At the beginning of the novel they have brainwashed Bond and installed him at the Ritz to assassinate M with what is effectively a water pistol filled with cyanide.

As ever with the enemies of Britain however, they are not quite able to fathom the national psyche, and get Bond ever so slightly wrong. In *From Russia with Love* there is the incredulity with which the Russians regard the devotion of the English agent, who works without special privileges, yet with great devotion. "It is perhaps the Public School and University tradition," muses General Vozdishenskyo touchingly.

The Soviets never could quite understand the British way – and even though Bond is of Scottish and Swiss descent he is essentially British. Distinctions are drawn in *The Man with the Golden Gun*, where the characteristic behaviour of the "real" Bond, as opposed to the brainwashed Soviet stooge, is outlined by M's chief of staff, elsewhere described as Bond's best friend in the service: "The Ritz is sort of 'stage' Bond. And these new clothes. Why did he have to bother? Doesn't matter what he was wearing when he came in through Dover. Normal thing, if he was in rags, would have been to give me a ring – he had my home number – and get me to fix him up."

The key to the Bond style will always elude his enemies, not merely because, at least in the novels, the mystique of Bond must remain intact and impenetrable for him

(*Opposite, far left*) The faceless bureaucrats of Whitehall were very much part of the Cold War climate and the "closed" government of the day

(*Opposite, left*) The appointed tailor for Winchester school in the Fifties. Part of the private school system was its sartorial traditions, a dress code by which old boys could recognize one another – and if need be, unmask imposters

(*Right*) Officers of the Guards in civilian dress, marching to a ceremony in London, 1958

to remain a hero. His body may be mutilated in the most terrible ways, take for instance his particularly gruesome time at the hands of Le Chiffre in *Casino Royale*, who uses a seatless chair and a carpet beater to the most horrific effect, but the style, the essence, of the man cannot be harmed. The message is clear: even after 12 novels and a number of short stories, Bond cannot be copied. One can buy a man a blue suit, a white shirt, a knitted silk tie, install him at the Ritz and presumably instruct him in how to order expensive wine and food, but these parts do not add up to the whole James Bond.

For all its apparent simplicity the style of Bond is an elusive thing. In *Moonraker*, Bond prepares himself for an evening at Blades thus: "in a heavy white silk shirt, dark blue trousers of navy serge, dark blue socks and well polished moccasin shoes, he was sitting at his desk, with a pack of cards in one hand and Scarne's wonderful guide to cheating open in front of him." After half an hour he "went into his bedroom, filled the wide black case with cigarettes and slipped it into his hip pocket, put on a black knitted silk tie and his jacket and verified that his chequebook was in his note case." These, along with the ageing black and white hound's-tooth suit and the dark blue sea-island cotton shirts which, together with the black leather sandals and navy blue tropical worsted trousers, make up his casual attire, are the simple sartorial essentials of James Bond.

There is of course a "faded black windcheater" to slip on when it comes to knocking a golf ball about, and a "thin, double-ended, black satin tie" to wear with the "single-

NICK FOULKES

James Bond, dressed for dinner,
discusses the merits of a
particular brandy with Colonel
Smithers (Richard Vernon), an
official of the Bank of England,
in *Goldfinger*, 1964

Bond's visits to M's wood-paneled office, as in *Goldfinger*,
were always something of an occasion worth dressing up
for, as usually the imminent fate of the world was about to
be put into his hands

(*Left*) Bond, undercover as an executive for Universal Exports in *From Russia With Love*, wears a lightweight suit, whose cut, along with the curled brim trilby hat, gives him the look of a travelling businessman

(*Opposite*) Bond at the Kiss-Kiss Club in *Thunderball*, 1965 goes looking for SPECTRE assassin, Fiona Volpe. Ian Fleming had a preference for lightweight suits, expressed in his books and developed in the films, which did much to promote their popularity

breasted dinner-jacket" and "heavy silk evening shirt" when the time comes to savour the "solid, studied comfort of card-rooms and casinos" and be "amused by the impartiality of the roulette ball and the playing cards – and their eternal bias." But the wardrobe of the Bond of the novels remains a small piece of furniture with but a few hangers in it; and the items suspended from its single rail become more familiar to the Bond aficionado than the clothes in his own closet.

What is interesting is that for all its pared-down qualities, Bond's wardrobe remains shadowy, the details indistinct. The shirts may be of silk, but the reader is never told where they were bought or what the collar looks like; the suits are from some nameless tailor and we do not know whether the jackets are two or three-button, whether the lapels are broad or narrow. Such considerations may seem those of a pedant but the ignorance in which the reader is left is made all the more plain by the detail in which Fleming luxuriates when describing the attire of his other male characters. It is almost as if Bond's appearance is some kind of sartorial *tabula rasa*, a neutral background which will throw the appearance of others into sharper relief, imbue it with enhanced significance.

Take for instance Bond's appraisal of Sir Hugo Drax, the villain in *Moonraker*. "Bond concluded his inspection with Drax's clothes which were expensive and in excellent taste,

James Bond not only travelled to what were then the most far-flung corners of the world (Japan in *You Only Live Twice*, 1967) but also knew just what to wear when he got there. In humid downtown Tokyo he wears a lightweight two-piece tailored for him by Anthony Sinclair of Conduit Street, Mayfair

a dark blue pinstripe in lightweight flannel, double-breasted with turnback cuffs, a heavy white silk shirt with a stiff collar, an unobtrusive tie with a small grey and white check, modest cuff links, which looked like Cartier, and a plain gold Patek Philippe watch with a black leather strap." In this one paragraph the reader is told more about Drax's incarnation as the consummate man of taste than he ever learns about Bond's choice of clothes. Just what sort of cuff links does 007 wear?

Having James Bond's personal style so shadowily defined has its uses. The implied phlegmatic elegance of Bond contrasts with the style of the sadistic loudmouth Milton Krest, the villain in *The Hildebrand Rarity*. "He looked hard and fit, and the faded blue jeans, military-cut shirt and wide leather belt suggested that he made a fetish of doing so – looking tough… Bond ran his eyes down the man from the sparse close-cropped black and grey hair, like iron filings sprinkled over the bullet head, to the tattooed eagle above a fouled anchor on the right forearm and then down to the naked leathery feet that stood nautically on the carpet. He thought: this man looks like a Hemingway hero. I'm not going to get on with him."

There is enough rigour, almost Calvinism, no doubt due to that Scottish and Swiss ancestry, about Bond's style for him to be able to take a morally superior stance when faced with excessive dandyism. Take his appraisal of the prevailing "Edwardian Look" of the late Fifties and early Sixties, as modelled by Dr Fanshawe, a Fabergé expert in *The Property of a Lady*: "The stranger was middle-aged, rosy, well fed and clothed rather foppishly in the neo-Edwardian fashion – turnback cuffs to his dark blue, four-buttoned jacket, a pearl pin in a heavy silk cravat, spotless wing collar, cuff links formed from what appeared to be antique coins, pince-nez on a thick black ribbon. Bond summed him up as something literary, a critic perhaps, a bachelor – possibly with homosexual tendencies."

Bond's fears, not about the "homosexual tendencies", rather the neo-Edwardian's artistic bent, are borne out and the man is made the butt of M's merciless philistinism – which is portrayed as a laudable quality in the face of so much dubious scholarship. M is actually rather proud of the fact that as a naval officer he has had neither the time nor the money to acquire works of art – although he has of course had the time to paint watercolours of orchids and collect the cutlasses which decorate his Grace and Favour Regency manor house on the edge of Windsor forest, and the money to join an expensive gaming club, namely Blades.

M, a sort of Victorian patriarch in a stiff white collar and loosely tied spotted bow tie, disapproves of many other things too. Among his list of *bêtes noires* are suntans, men with beards, people who are completely bilingual, people who try to bring pressure on

(*Far left*) The dapper Alan Bates, social-climbing hero of *Nothing But the Best*, 1964, resplendent in bowler hat, stiff cutaway collar and velvet trimmed overcoat

(*Left*) Patrick MacNee as John Steed in *The Avengers*; another well dressed Englishman – but one whose style went deliberately over the top

him with family connections or friendship with Cabinet ministers, Bond's womanizing, Bond's taste for vodka martinis – a drink he dismisses as "rot-gut" – and of course men and women who are too dressy. M himself preferring simple square-cut blue suits. Given Bond's almost unswerving devotion to this crotchety old sailor, it is reasonable to assume that some of his boss's tastes inform Bond's own personal style.

This asceticism also neatly allows him to take the moral high ground when faced with the luxury of the international playboy as personified by Count Lippe in *Thunderball*. "He was an athletic-looking six foot, dressed in the sort of casually well-cut beige herringbone tweed that suggests Anderson & Sheppard. He wore a white silk shirt and a dark red polka-dot tie and the soft dark brown V-necked sweater looked like vicuña." The fact that Count Lippe, incidentally the driver of a violet Bentley, is not just wearing a jacket redolent of any old Savile Row tailor, but one which is known – to those who know these things – for the relaxed, unstructured type of coat favoured by the Duke of Windsor, and his sweater is not just made of any old wool, but the fleece of a rare, tawny-coloured South American mammal, leads Bond to an inevitable conclusion: Lippe is "a good-looking bastard who got all the women he wanted and probably lived on them – and lived well."

For Bond, style and an understanding of it are useful tools of the secret agent, not just a vanity. It is a little like the Rolex watch he wears in *On Her Majesty's Secret Service*,

(*Right*) The Duke of Windsor, with the Duchess, in England, October 1946, wearing one of his favourite sports jackets

(*Far right*) SPECTRE agent, Count Lippe (Guy Doleman) in *Thunderball* whose comfortable-looking tweed jacket belies his murderous intentions for Bond

and uses as a knuckle-duster; not merely a rich man's bauble, but something which can be pressed into useful service.

In order to find out more about Count Lippe he breaks into his room at Shrublands: "All he learned – from the clothes – was that the count was a much travelled man – shirts from Charvet, ties from Tripler, Dior and Hardy Amies, shoes from Peal, and raw silk pyjamas from Hong Kong." A sartorial snapshot which neatly places him "as a tough maquereau from the Ritz bar in Paris, the Palace at St Moritz, the Carlton at Cannes – good at backgammon, polo, water-skiing, but with the yellow streak of the man who lives on women." Yet Lippe is also the sort of man who can carry out acts of violence swiftly and coolly. There is the impression that the Shrublands episode, almost completely incidental to the main narrative thrust of the book, was introduced merely to allow Fleming to have some fun with the dietary fads of the time and, with the character of Lippe, speculate as to the sort of man Bond might be were he to abandon himself totally to the world of polo and backgammon, the Carlton and the Ritz.

For although Bond may enjoy Taittinger Blanc de Blancs Brut '43 and caviar, tankards of pink champagne and the sweet tender meat of stone crabs, he also appreciates the hearty taste of a hunk of Lyon sausage and half a litre of Macon with the cork pulled, the garlic flavour of Strasbourg sausage with a bottle of Pisse-de-chat (the irreverent nickname for "a passable Riquewihr") or a double portion of "matjes herrings

(*Opposite*) Stylish as always, Fleming on a visit to one of the locations for *From Russia With Love*, wears a white cashmere crew neck and carries a cherished gadget – a walking stick with a leather-covered handle, which opens up to form an instant seat

Emilio Largo's monogrammed silk dressing gown contrasts villainously with Bond's preference for his trademark towelling. Adolfo Celi and Claudine Auger on the deck of the Disco Volante, in *Thunderball*, 1965

The first James Bond story, *Casino Royale*, was published in 1953 and the Americans, scenting a winner, irreverently transformed him into a CIA agent, 'Jimmy Bond', for a 1954 black and white TV play. Barry Nelson, the first actor to play the part was kitted out in a loose-fitting shawl collared tuxedo, and what looks suspiciously like a clip-on bow tie

The cover art of these two PAN paperbacks, both published within a few years of each other, illustrate the difficulty in determining the most likely age of James Bond

THE STYLE SECRETS OF JAMES BOND

(*Top and bottom left*) During the planning of the *Daily Express* cartoon strip, Ian Fleming commissioned his own artist's impression of James Bond as a guide to how he saw his hero. The cartoon strip artist, John McLusky, felt it was far too 'pre-war' in spirit and gave his own Bond a much more aggressively masculine look

The 1958 poster announcing the start of the new James Bond strip cartoon in the *Daily Express*, drawn by John McLusky proved hugely popular with the readers and boosted the circulation of the newspaper

smothered in cream onion rings" accompanied by doubles of schnapps and draught Lowenbrau.

He quickly tires of living high, soft and easy, as the opening chapters of *Goldfinger* show. This book also allows a wonderful sartorial sketch of another international type. "Mr Du Pont was about 50 – pink, clean-shaven and dressed in the conventional disguise with which Brooks Brothers cover the shame of American millionaires. He wore a single-breasted dark tan tropical suit and a white silk shirt with a shallow collar. The rolled ends of the collar were joined by a gold safety pin beneath the knot of a narrow dark red and blue striped tie that fractionally wasn't the Brigade of Guards'. The cuffs of the shirt protruded half an inch below the cuffs of the coat and showed cabochon crystal links containing miniature trout flies. The socks were charcoal-grey silk and the shoes were old and polished mahogany and hinted Peal. The man carried a dark, narrow-brimmed straw homburg with a wide claret ribbon."

As Anthony Burgess remarked, "it is the mastery of things rather than people that gives Fleming his particular literary niche." And it is indeed not to a James Bond novel that one would turn for insight into the tortured workings of the human soul, for blinding penetration into the human condition. But when it comes to "things", Fleming is the nonpareil. A naked man, an assassin in *From Russia with Love*, is identified by a pile of belongings at his side: a money clip made of a Mexican $50 piece stuffed with banknotes, a gold Dunhill lighter, a Fabergé cigarette case, an old P. G. Wodehouse novel and Girard-Perregaux moonphase watch. All "typical membership badges of the rich man's club." Meanwhile a fellow secret service agent is tacitly condemned for wearing the old school tie, that of a Wykehamist, drinking tea and smoking "Kent filter-tips through – he was a careful man – a Dunhill filter holder."

Clothes are always telling but with his eye for detail Fleming is also able to turn something as mundane as tobacco, and its use, into a barometer of character. Bond is allowed the eccentric connoisseurship of his Morland Specials with their triple gold rings, and offers his opinion on pretty much every other brand of cigarette the world has to offer, when, as must often be the case with a man who has a 60- or 70-a-day habit, he runs out of his favourite brand. In *You Only Live Twice* he is introduced to the Japanese brand Shinsei. "He took a cigarette and lit it. It burned rapidly with something of the effect of a slow-burning firework. It had a vague taste of American blends, but it was good and sharp on the lungs like 90° proof spirits. He let the smoke out in a quiet hiss and smiled."

Pipe-smoking is seen as solid, if slightly old-fashioned. M is always filling his pipe, tamping it down and getting it going. And Pleydell-Smith, the Colonial Secretary in *Dr*

The *Daily Express* strip cartoons remained remarkably close to Ian Fleming's novels and short stories, and laid the visual groundwork for the films

Two James Bonds with the same car, the Aston Martin DB5 – for years, many schoolboys' most dreamt-about vehicle.

Bond's wardrobe always worked best when it reflected his military background and the need to be smartly turned out at all times. In *Goldfinger*, Sean Connery wears a tweed hacking jacket, plain cotton shirt, plain tie and heavy weight cavalry twill trousers, with cross pockets and narrow bottoms, angled to fit neatly over his suede "chukka" boots.

Pierce Brosnan, over 30 years later, also echos the off-duty military look in *GoldenEye*, in a navy blue cable knit sweater, silk foulard cravat, narrow-leg cotton moleskin trousers and Church's brown brogues

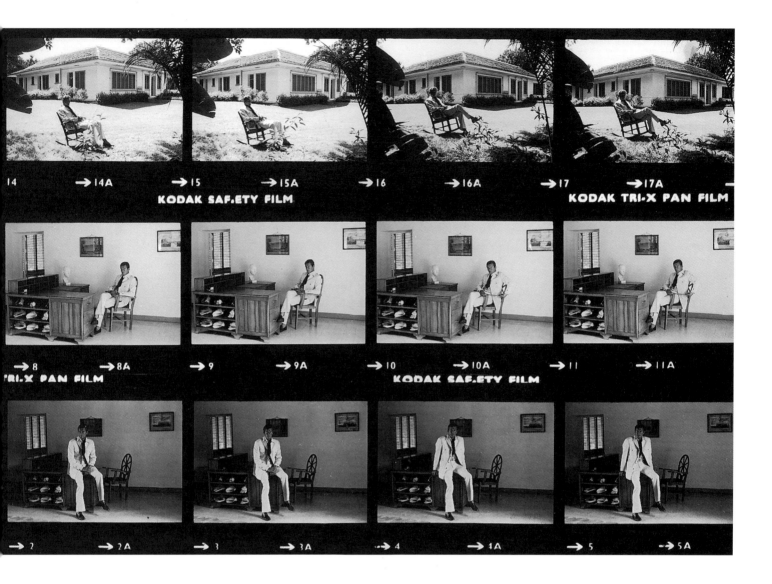

No, is recognized by Bond to be "an ally, and an intelligent one at that" after having done little more than play with his pipe and dig into a tobacco jar bearing the arms of King's College Cambridge.

Cigars, however, are a very different matter. At their best they are merely a totem of the Establishment, as smoked by the colonial governor who tells the Maugham-like story in *Quantum of Solace*, and offered by Porterfield, the club servant, at Blades. The cheroots smoked by M are an indulgence – and are probably as nasty as "the Infuriator", the disgusting Algerian wine he swears by. But when smoked by Drax, who enjoys not just a cigar, not just a Havana, but a cabinet-quality Havana, cigars take on an air of decadent menace. Scaramanga too has a sinister, theatrical way of smoking the cheroots he extracts from his expensive cigar case – he "let the smoke dribble out between his lips and

Roger Moore visited Fleming's Jamaican home Goldeneye
in 1973, during the filming of *Live and Let Die*, to absorb
some of the atmosphere of the birthplace of Bond

inhaled the thin stream up his nostrils" – and Largo uses a Corona cigar in conjunction with ice cubes to torture Domino Vitali in *Thunderball.*

Thus the Bond style evolves and emerges throughout the books, each experience adding another level of complexity to the tastes, appetites, preferences and prejudices that together form 007. It is an indication of the skilful way that Fleming handles the world of "things" that Bond may be right to distrust a man who fastens his tie with a Windsor knot, even though the reader is never told how James Bond knots his own tie.

Such details are telling, subtle and every bit as effective as, say, the collar-stud incident in E. M. Forster's *A Passage to India. Soi-disant* literary critics may sneer at Fleming's infatuation with appearance and branded goods, but before they curl their lip too much they might do well to consult their no doubt well-thumbed copy of Proust's *A Remembrance of Things Past*, where at one point the narrator occupies himself "tightening from time to time the knot of my magnificent Charvet tie and taking care not to soil my polished boots." At another point Proust describes Swann's hair as being "done in the Bressant style", after a famous nineteenth-century actor who introduced the wearing of hair short at the front and long at the back. Surely it is not too far-fetched to recall descriptions of Bond in the early books, with his unruly comma of hair, a little in the style of Hoagy Carmichael, a description he incidentally refutes, preferring the epithet "piratical".

Parallels with Proust are of course ambitious and are probably the last thing Ian Fleming himself would have wanted, but nevertheless each man has – in his own way and in his own genre, one with Swann, the other with Bond – contributed to the sort of literature which relies on and sharpens people's perception and understanding of the material world. The difficulty would be in how best to transfer the James Bond of the books, a man for whom another's brand of tie, and how he tied it was pregnant with significance and whose own style was classic, correct and timeless – but never described in detail – to the screen.

DISGUISES

It is perhaps fortunate that disguises have been kept to a minimum in the films, since more often than not they simply don't work, and Bond is discovered. As Telly Savalas's Blofeld tells him in *On Her Majesty's Secret Service*, "It takes more than glasses and a hat to turn James Bond into a herald". Moreover, it is Bond's blend of guile and sheer cheek which thrills us and endears us to him, rather than don a false moustache, it is far more his style to slip in the back way, climb in over the roof, or else just walk in through the front door and present himself at reception.

Disguises, one feels, are a little beneath Bond, and they tend to be played for laughs: it is hard to take George Lazenby's bekilted impersonation of Sir Hilary Bray, or Roger Moore in Arab garb, completely seriously. Sean Connery's lavish Japanese wedding in *You Only Live Twice* finds him in a deeply unconvincing disguise, especially his fringe and temporary oriental eyes, the stare threatening to upset the whole balance of the film.

It is ironical that Timothy Dalton, a theatrically trained actor used to doublet and hose, looked, if anything, more comfortable in his Mujaheddin costume than he did in his suits.

OVER AND UNDER

Skiing's adrenaline rush made a swift convert of Ian Fleming, who learnt at Kitzbühel, between school and Sandhurst, years before the sport became fashionable. He was known as a fearless, if unorthodox skier, and of course wished the sport onto his creation Bond. Style-wise, in *On Her Majesty's Secret Service*, George Lazenby manages to borrow a smart sky-blue two-piece Spandex ski suit, goggles and white roll-neck as well as his skis, for his moonlight descent from Piz Gloria, pursued by Blofeld's orange and black-clad goons, and Roger Moore found a Union Jack parachute a useful accessory after skiing off a 3,000ft cliff in *The Spy Who Loved Me*.

In *For Your Eyes Only* Moore wears ski gear by Willy Bogner – a veteran Olympic downhill ace – who, as well as having shot Lazenby's bobsleigh chase with Telly Savalas earlier, was also the specialist cameraman for the snow action in the film, and the later Arctic teaser scene in *A View to a Kill*.

Meanwhile, beneath the waves, Scuba diving (from the "Self Contained Underwater Breathing Apparatus" developed towards the end of World War II) was much slower to catch on as a leisure activity. Despite the splendid underwater films of Jacques Cousteau and others, scuba diving retained an air of military menace and individual danger, partially fuelled by the 1957 discovery of the headless corpse of the freelance frogman Commander Crabb. He had been on a covert mission to inspect the hull of the Soviet cruiser 'Ordzhonikze', which had brought Kruschev and Bulganin to Portsmouth, and must have been caught and killed by an underwater patrol, similar to Largo's wet-suited and trident armed team. The arrival in *Thunderball* of the American cavalry in the form of the American Navy SEALs, the heady mix of orange rubber, big black zips, Claudine Auger and James Bond can probably be said to have been a changing point for recreational scuba diving worldwide.

BATH, BED AND BEYOND

Getting wet and getting dried again has always been a popular activity throughout the series, guaranteeing an important role for that most functional of fabrics – cotton towelling.

The impressive amount of time which Bond has spent in Turkish baths, health resorts, bedrooms and bathrooms – plus his championing of the unisex bathrobe – must have placed the entire world towelling industry in his debt. Nevertheless, their success might have been short-lived if the now notorious baby blue romper suit from *Goldfinger* had ever appeared more than once.

Robes have come in big checks, broad stripes and some long, some short, as well as traditional piped cotton dressing gowns, worn, occasionally, with that most under-used item in his suitcase – silk pyjamas. Even when no help from the wardrobe department was at hand, Bond could always be relied upon to fold a bath-towel with military precision.

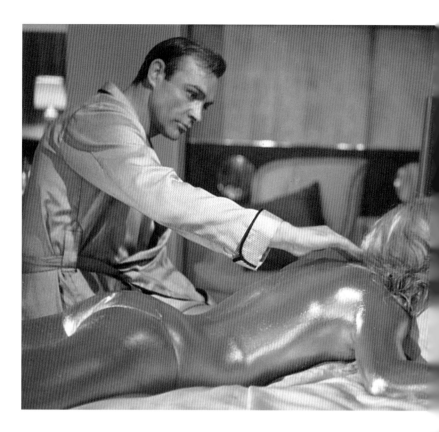

George Sanders, as Leslie Charteris's *The Saint* stars as one of the cinema's first reluctantly-armed civilians to be entrusted with the knightly pursuit of ideals and the protection of individual freedoms

THE RETURN
OF THE SUITED HERO

Neil Norman

 f James Bond was the last great screen hero to wear a suit, when did the suited hero fall from fashion?

Once upon a time, heroes wore armour and chain mail. It afforded a certain amount of protection against the slings, arrows and napalm breath of the foes, human and mythical, which they were obliged to fight. But as time went on, and automobiles superseded stallions, the hero required a softer, more wearer-friendly casing in which to perform his deeds of selfless courage.

Enter the hero in a suit. In the first decades of the cinema, the suit was the only acceptable dress for the prototypical screen hero. It betokened reliability, trustworthiness, elegance of body and also mind, cleanliness and athleticism. It lent the wearer the air of someone who could take care of himself and, by association, others. Suits were the mark of the professional.

Time was – in the Thirties, Forties, Fifties, Sixties and early Seventies – when the hero would not be seen in anything other than a correctly cut, impeccably tailored suit. Nearly five decades in which every male hero, from George Sanders as The Saint, through William Powell as Dashiell Hammett's gentleman sleuth hero in *The Thin Man*, to James Coburn as *Our Man Flint* (one of several ersatz Bonds) fought, quipped and shot their way effortlessly through heroic deeds. Often they came in pairs: Robert Vaughn and David McCallum, the men from U.N.C.L.E., Robert Culp and Bill Cosby of *I-Spy*.

Of course, in the days before casualwear and the insidious sportswear invaded the male wardrobe – and thence the costume departments of film production companies – suits and formal attire were worn by hero and villain alike. For every detective, FBI agent or gentleman sleuth that strode across the screen, shooting his cuffs as often as his revolver, there was a sharply dressed criminal to oppose him. Sadly for the heroes of the gangster melodramas of the Thirties, the villains' access to copious amounts of money ensured their sartorial superiority.

Thus, Edward G. Robinson's Little Caesar, James Cagney's Public Enemy and George Raft's "Spats" Columbo represented the cutting edge of gangster chic – heavy-

(*Left*) William Powell as Dashiell Hammett's 1930's gentleman sleuth in *The Thin Man*

(*Below*) David McCallum, as Ilya Kuryakin, the other man from U.N.C.L.E., 1964-1968

(*Left*) Robert Stack, as Eliot Ness in the TV series of *The Untouchables*, always went well-armed with waistcoat and fedora

(*Opposite*) James Coburn as *Our Man Flint*, 1966, one of Hollywood's answers to Bond, also knew how to look after his leading ladies, here Gila Golan

weight double-breasted suits coupled with high-waisted trousers that assisted the arrogant swagger of the well-dressed career villain.

Curiously, the heroes of the period and the following decades of the Forties and Fifties, while attired in suits, were often a little dowdy, unless they were cast in an exotic location. The difference between Humphrey Bogart's suited hero Sam Spade in *The Maltese Falcon* and the white tuxedoed Rick Blaine in *Casablanca* is all too evident – Spade is a rumpled private eye whose suit has seen better days, while Rick is an impeccable exile, presenting an altogether classier image.

There are, of course, honourable exceptions. William Powell in the *Thin Man* series was the epitome of the well-dressed gentleman sleuth and was rarely to be seen out of a perfectly tailored lounge suit, or evening dress – usually accompanied by a martini glass and a cigarette. The air of amused decadence that clung to him was a throwback to the Twenties and he operated in a leisured, cultured and privileged climate of sophistication and lacerating wit.

A similar combination of sophisticated urbanity and playful ennui accompanied Cary Grant in many of his films during the Forties, when, dressed to the hilt, he played havoc among the socialites in *The Awful Truth*, *Bringing Up Baby*, *My Favourite Wife*, *His Girl Friday* and *The Philadelphia Story*, before entering true hero mode in *North by Northwest* and *Charade*.

As Cagney and Robinson had done before him, the diminutive Alan Ladd had his suits cleverly tailored to give the illusion of height. Throughout his films, notably *The Blue Dahlia*, *This Gun for Hire*, and *The Glass Key*, the fact of his being suited materially assisted his heroic status.

Many studio portraits of the time depict such screen idols as Gregory Peck, Gary Cooper, Montgomery Clift, Robert Mitchum and Clark Gable in beautifully tailored suits, cut from a heavy cloth which enhanced the depth of focus and softened the edges of their profiles. Mitchum's amusing dictum, that his acting style was simply to point his suit in the right direction, may have been closer to the truth than was once supposed.

But then, for a number of reasons, the suited hero began to wane. Social, political and cultural associations began to attach themselves to the suit which went against the grain of the developing screen hero. After a while, the suit became synonymous with institutionalized heroics; good guys in suits were increasingly members of such organizations as the FBI or the CIA, MI5 and MI6. The suit equalled the Establishment, and as the typical screen hero became increasingly anti-Establishment, the suit began to drift off the shoulders of the heroes and onto the backs of the villains.

Gangster chic, with waistcoat and watchchain:
Edward G. Robinson as *Little Caesar*, proves that
villains can afford better tailors

(*Opposite*) Cutting edge of bad-guy styling: George Raft became "Spats" Columbo, with long pointed collars and the widest lapels of the era

Jean Harlow, Edward Woods and James Cagney in *Public Enemy*, 1931

(*Left*) Cary Grant's sophisticated urbanity contrasts with Jimmy Stewart's more relaxed style, with Ruth Hussey, in *The Philadelphia Story*, 1940

(*Above*) Not all leading men were six-foot tall. Alan Ladd, even shorter here in *The Blue Dahlia*, 1945, had his suits tailored to give him height

(*Left*) Gregory Peck, with patterned tie and white silk handkerchief, poses for this studio portrait to promote *The Macomber Affair*, 1947

(*Opposite*) Bogart in *Casablanca* anticipates the Bondian appeal of white tuxedos in exotic locations

(*Opposite*) Gary
Cooper and his
million-dollar profile,
in *Fountainhead*,
1948

(*Right*) Robert
Mitchum's rumpled
role in the 1975 re-
make of *Farewell My
Lovely* marks a
downturn in the
fortunes of the
suited hero, which
may have begun as
far back as Bogart's
'Sam Spade'

Harrison Ford dresses down in the first of the Indiana Jones
adventures, *Raiders of the Lost Ark*, 1981, while Paul Freeman
who plays the villainous Frenchman, Belloq, smartly turned out
in a tropical linen suit

(*Right*) Bruce Willis, whose overpumped muscles gave him a vested interest in the decline of the suit in film. *Die Hard*, 1988

(*Below*) The real turning-point: Bruce Willis's blue-collar hero John McClane sweats it out against Alan Rickman's Hans Gruber, all European elegance, in *Die Hard*, 1988

A velvet collar too far. Patrick MacNee's John Steed in *The Avengers*, 1967-1969

Somewhere around the Seventies, when fashion interfered with finesse, suits started to appear ridiculous: wide lapels, flared trousers and unsuitable materials all connived to destroy the credibility of the wearer. Heroes looked more like rock stars in civvies. Bond fever was cooling slightly, Roger Moore was getting older, taking Fleming's immortal hero with him into an age of corsetry. The suit was no longer sexy attire for a hero. It was either too formal and stiff or too susceptible to the vagaries of fashion. The concept of the suited hero performing deeds of derring-do in a crumple-free, crease-resistant suit was outmoded. It was no longer the mark of the stylish individual hero but of either the corporate yes-man or the undercover yob.

So what did our heroes turn to? They dressed down, the look was rough and ready. Leather jackets and chinos, jeans and T-shirts were the order of the day. And the hero who wrought the change was Indiana Jones.

The arrival of Harrison Ford as Indy in the first – and best – of the Spielberg/Lucas adventures, *Raiders of the Lost Ark* (1981), although in a Forties setting, heralded the death of the suited hero. Or at least put him in a coma. Indy's adventures were so action-packed, the inference was that suits would simply not stand up to the strain of being dragged beneath the wheels of speeding trucks, rolling down hillsides, ducking spears, bullets, arrows etc.

At the same time, a curious thing happened. The suit wouldn't die. It simply transferred its allegiance from hero to villain. Paul Freeman's villainous Frenchman, Belloq, in *Raiders*, confronted Indy in an immaculate linen suit. And the moment that Alan Rickman as Hans Gruber strode on to the screen in *Die Hard* (1988) to do battle with Bruce Willis's slobbily attired cop hero, villainy meant tailoring sharp enough to slash your wrists on.

There was a class agenda at work here too. Snobbery with violence, as Noel Coward once dubbed the James Bond movies, gave way to a New Proletarianism. Heroes stepped down from their pedestals where they had been since Conan Doyle and Buchan, all the way through to Leslie Charteris's Simon Templar and television's John Steed. Villains went in the opposite direction and began to ascend the social scale.

Suddenly the best-dressed men on the screen were kidnapping heroines, inflicting all manner of diabolical cruelty and issuing lethal admonitions and ultimatums. Style and fastidiousness became watchwords for villainy. Paul Freeman's Belloq wears his linen suit and panama with the fluid grace of one born to style, echoing the white-suited heroes (and villains) of the past: Paul Henried in *Casablanca*, Carlos Thompson in television's *The Sentimental Agent*, Caesar Romero, Sydney Greenstreet, to name but a few.

Retro suit action: Robert Redford's *The Great Gatsby*, 1974

(*Left*) Kevin Costner took up Eliot
Ness's waistcoat, hat and holster
for the 1987 film version of *The
Untouchables*

(*Below*) Jack Nicholson and Faye Dunaway
in *Chinatown*, 1974. An important 'suit'
movie for both of them

Since the Seventies heroic suit exceptions have been found, more often than not, in period pieces. Robert Redford's *The Great Gatsby* (1974), and Jack Nicholson's *Chinatown* (1974) are important suit movies. *The Untouchables* (1987) reacquainted us with Eliot Ness and his Federal Agent gangbusters, featuring Kevin Costner wearing a Prohibition-period suit with aplomb.

The Eighties was the decade of suit revolution. Suits became untrustworthy. They completed the transition from heroic symbol to symbol of deceit, treachery and danger. Suits belonged on the backs of sharp lawyers, Wall Street brokers, corporate pirates, advertising executives. As boom accelerated towards bust, the ambivalence towards these characters became more marked. It reached its apotheosis in Gordon Gekko, Michael Douglas's monster of avarice, who capsized the movie *Wall Street*. Written as the villain, Douglas played it with such potency and relish that he was unwittingly perceived as the hero, wielding the unassailable power of intellect, hedonism and greed.

Double-breasted power suits – a return to the gangster chic of the 1930s – worn with alarmingly red braces and wingtip brogues, became the armour of Gekko and the other new knights of this financial Camelot. These were heroes on the cusp of villainy.

As suits drifted further away from actual attire and towards pure symbolism, filmmakers with a satirical postmodern take on wardrobe took up the stage to make statements. Thus in John Landis's *The Blues Brothers* the heroes are defined by their skinny two-piece single-breasted suits with bumfreezer jackets and pork-pie hats. Later, the gang members of *Reservoir Dogs* went to work in identical black suits, white shirts and black ties. Professional criminals to a T, they looked like a cross between FBI agents and undertakers.

Running parallel with the evolution of the suit as heroic attire is the evolution of the handgun. In the days when small arms meant just that, a revolver could be slipped into a pocket and the suit would not bulge unnecessarily. When Sean Connery or Roger Moore went into action it was with a Walther PPK, a firearm selected as much for its discreet, slim shape as for its effective stopping power. As weapons became increasingly large, it became more and more difficult to conceal them with any degree of stylistic finesse beneath a suit jacket.

We can probably lay the blame at the door of Clint Eastwood's Dirty Harry Callaghan, whose .44 Magnum was "the most powerful handgun in the world and liable to blow your head clean off." Unfortunately it was liable to ruin the line of a perfectly good suit too. Heroes became increasingly concerned with the size of their artillery, until stars of the nature of Sylvester Stallone and Arnold Schwarzenegger – whose pumped-up torsoes ensured that they looked absurd in suits anyway – gave up the idea of wearing holsters and began toting holdalls loaded with guns as oversized as their pectorals.

Greed is good and red braces too. Michael Douglas's Gordon Gekko
spells out the rules of corporate morality to a Cerruti-suited Charlie
Sheen, *Wall Street*, 1987

(*Opposite*) The eclipse of the suited hero may owe something to the need to carry bigger and bigger handguns. Clint Eastwood's 'Dirty Harry' Callaghan, 1974, achieved some success in concealing his .44 Magnum by wearing badly-fitting tweed jackets – until, a decade later – Rambo's arm-held machine guns finally put paid to wearing much more on top than muscles and crossed bandoliers

(*Above*) Dan Aykroyd and John Belushi in *The Blues Brothers*, 1980: bumfreezer jackets, Slim Jim ties, stingy-brim hats and shades

(*Right*) Mr Black and his similarly suited colleagues go to work in *Reservoir Dogs*, 1993

The combined effect of unshaven, muscle-bound heroes, bigger ordnance and the general shift towards unsubtle, bludgeoning heroes coincided with the increasing suspicion in which men of elegance and good grooming were held. In an era when overfastidiousness suggested potential criminality, the ultimate hero/villain turned up in the shape of Richard Gere in *American Gigolo*. Here was Man in Armani, who combined contemporary taste with the morals of an alley cat. The suit became an extension of male vanity – and vanity cannot be the chief characteristic of any hero.

Similarly, the overall decline in language, wit and dialogue accompanied the decline in male attire. The four-letter words, oaths and street imprecations with which modern screenwriters are increasingly obsessed do not sit well upon the lips of an elegant, manicured, well-dressed man. On the contrary the heroes of old – partly due to the Hays Office, partly due to the fact that some of the most prestigious writers alive worked for Hollywood – spoke with an elegance and wit that was in keeping with their mode of dress.

(*Opposite and right*)
Having personally
killed off the suited
hero in *Raiders*,
Harrison Ford
involuntarily brings
him back to life as CIA
agent Jack Ryan in
Patriot Games, 1992
and *Clear and Present
Danger*, 1994

NEIL NORMAN

Never knowingly underdressed, Pierce Brosnan's 1995 Bond
wears a three-piece suit for his visit to company headquarters
and then down to Q's Department in the basement

But whether we consider the heroes of Hollywood or those of the European cinema, the fact remains that the suited hero has achieved an immortality beyond the dreams of the scruffy oiks of the last decade and a half. Cary Grant and David Niven, Robert Mitchum and William Powell, Ronald Colman, Clark Gable, Gary Cooper and Montgomery Clift, Charles Boyer, George Sanders, Claude Rains, Robert Taylor, and later, Robert Redford, Jack Nicholson, Alain Delon, Marcello Mastroianni and Jean-Louis Trintignant. All have at some time in their careers occupied the honourable position of the hero in a suit.

Ironically, Harrison Ford, whose character Indiana Jones was largely contributive to taking heroes out of suits, put them back inside them as Jack Ryan, Tom Clancy's hero of *Patriot Games* and *Clear and Present Danger*. The former CIA agent forecasts the return of the suited hero. Here was a man who could dodge mortar and bazooka attacks in Bogota and stay alive to brush the debris from his suit.

And so to James Bond. Bond is a hero of refinement. His attire is as much a symbol of what he represents as a reflection of his own personal style. The well-tailored suit is to Bond the armour of his profession. And the better the tailoring, the more effective the armour. If only the victim in Hitchcock's *Saboteur* had patronized a better tailor, he might not have plunged to his death from the Statue of Liberty as a result of an uncertain jacket seam.

The trick of tailoring for James Bond is to give him a look that is essentially, though not aggressively, British. Classic, with a twist of international flair ensures that he can move easily from Whitehall offices to Turkish bordellos; from a Bajan beach to Monte Carlo casino. To witness the return of the suited hero in *GoldenEye* is to greet an old friend who has been absent for too long.

The standard army fatigue-inspired clothing championed by the most recent screen heroes has never looked anything but drab. The leather jackets, shapeless chinos and jeans, the vests, T-shirts or shirts without ties, the trainers and combat boots are all now regulation wear; they have themselves become institutionalized. From Mel Gibson to Bruce Willis, Martin Riggs to John McClane, all the big screen heroes look the same. There is no distinction, no investment of thought or care into grooming and appearance.

But it appears that the pendulum is swinging back. Heroes ought not to look as if they are on weekend leave from the army; they should dress to kill, but up, not down. Being a hero is a serious business: the hero's attitude and sense of self-respect should be reflected in his mode of dress.

It is time for heroes to be respected. Time for the civilizing influence of the suit. Time for heroes to be cool once again.

In post-war Britain, most demobilised soldiers were issued with the same style of double-breasted suit, cut from a very limited range of heavy, serviceable and instantly recognisable cloths. This created a new 'civilian' uniform and effectively killed off any chance of popularity for the style for nearly thirty years, leaving the single-breasted, two-piece suit to take over as the modern man's preferred choice, particularly for wearing in his now better-heated homes, offices and cars.

Apart from a brief appearance of Roger Moore's double-breasted suits in *Live and Let Die* and *The Man With The Golden Gun*, Bond always wears the two-piece style, unless he wants to make a real impression and then he chooses the added authority which a waistcoat gives.

In the Sixties, the three-piece suit was already becoming a symbol of the more conservative aspects of society and, being more expensive to make and sell, had gradually disappeared from the ready-to-wear racks in the shops.

Consequently, anyone wearing a three-piece suit automatically signalled that they probably stood for pre-war values and also still had the time and money to go to a tailor.

It is not surprising, then, that the earlier Bond occasionally wears a three-piece suit to help to transmit this immediate sense of status and independent financial means, whatever the prevailing fashion, and it has had a place in his wardrobe ever since.

GOOD SPORTS, BAD SPORTS

The British sports jacket looks its best in country tweeds with long vents and slanted side pockets, inherited from the practical needs of the riding coat. The smaller, now often vestigial, ticket pocket on the right hand side, a tailoring trick signifying a man of some financial standing, has been used to that effect from Connery through to Moore and is still subtly in evidence on Brosnan's *GoldenEye* suits.

Needless to say, it was Roger Moore who changed the sports jacket into a fashion item, as in his Donegal tweed, wide lapelled version with elbow patches in *Moonraker* and the narrow shouldered Texas-size check he wore with flared trousers in *The Man with the Golden Gun*.

Timothy Dalton's jackets were understated almost to vanishing point and Pierce Brosnan's – we assume he has one – has not as yet been seen in *GoldenEye*. However, like Bond, it will no doubt return.

BLAZING AWAY

Commander Bond, Royal Navy, is rarely seen in uniform, but a hint of the military man's attention to detail appears throughout the films and is well illustrated by the choice of his blazers – originally a short, practical marine coat, designed in the time of Nelson by the captain of H.M.S. Blazer as a uniform for his crew. It is a comfortable, stylish and adaptable garment, equally at home in M's office, taking part in an operational briefing, going out for tea or for bombing around Monte Carlo harbour in a powerboat. Roger Moore's version in *The Man with the Golden Gun* is virtually naval uniform without the braid, but it is left to that stylish Roman villain, Emilio Largo, to take the look one stage further, with his unusual eight-button version and a too-tight cut which, by Bond's standards, would automatically make him suspect.

TIES THAT BIND

Traditionally, well-dressed men – particularly James Bond – have preferred white, cream or pale blue shirts worn with plain or subtly patterned ties of the type which do not draw too much attention away from the face.

The films, following the sketchy details in the books, supplied James Bond with mainly slim, plain and knitted or textured silk ties to wear with his sea-island cotton or silk shirts from such London shirtmakers as Budd of the Piccadilly Arcade or Turnbull & Asser of Jermyn Street, whose turnback cuff style made its debut in *Dr No* and appeared consistently right through till *The Man with the Golden Gun*. Roger Moore championed the more dominant neckwear of the Seventies, which actually went with the period's higher, deeper collars and wider lapels.

The slim knitted black tie made a brief re-appearance on Timothy Dalton and anticipated the GoldenEye taste for the more traditional Jermyn Street look for Bond's collars and ties. On the subject of handkerchiefs, the squarely folded cotton lawn in the top pocket blended the need for some form of decoration with practicality – as at the beginning of *Dr No*. This style can be seen in all the early films being sported by both heroes and villains alike. Eventually all pocket handkerchiefs, symbols of a more elegant age, went out-of-fashion and out of film until Brosnan successfully re-adopts the very British, 'tucked-in' style for *GoldenEye* as yet another signal that the suited hero is back.

In the beginning: Sean Connery becomes James Bond in the first of cinema's longest running series, *Dr No*, winning the game and catching the eye of the player across the table

DRESSING THE PART

Nick Sullivan

Without the James Bond films, Britain's most famous secret agent would surely by now be another long-forgotten pulp fiction hero. For a time the John McLusky newspaper strips brought him fame, but were it not for "Cubby" Broccoli, Bond would have remained the cardboard booby that Fleming, frustrated at sluggish early book sales, called him, just another two-dimensional bruiser.

Fleming's taut, Chandleresque prose actually provided far more character detail than is sometimes realized, but it was the cinema which gave James Bond real depth, and most of what we know of 007 as modern myth comes from the films made by "Cubby" Broccoli's company, Eon Productions. This character-building was a compound process which began with *Dr No* in 1962, and each of the Bond films and the actors who played him have added to his identity. No other series of films has been so successful with the same central character: *GoldenEye* is the seventeenth in a sequence spanning over 30 years (will anyone know who Rambo was in 2020?) and, despite the vast changes through which he and his audiences have lived, Bond remains Britain's most charismatic film hero, his status as a male style icon largely undamaged; he always knew how to dress the part, although he did occasionally get it wrong.

Before the film of *Dr No*, if Bond was clear in Fleming's head he was still a rather ghostly figure to anyone who had merely read the books. While his enemies benefit from full-page introductions, physical and sartorial descriptions of Bond are kept to a minimum. Turning the somewhat elusive James Bond of the novels into the fully developed, instantly recognizable, highly stylized screen character was never going to be straightforward for the film makers. The creation of a viable style, consistent with the novels, capable of adapting according to changing tastes and still recognizable 34 years later, has been one of popular culture's great successes.

Although his style descriptions of Bond are tantalizingly sketchy, Fleming himself was very sure what 007 was like. He was like Fleming, or at least like the fictional character the writer would have wished to have been, as is clear to any reader of the handful of biographies now available. So much of Fleming's upbringing and education, his

(*Top left*) David Niven, archetypal upper-class English smoothie, Ian Fleming's close friend and his first choice for the part of James Bond; but he was already in his fifties, and not seen as tough enough

(*Top right*) Another original contender for the part: Richard Burton, here in pensive mood, might have brought too much of his own personality to the role

(*Right*) MGM's young star Roger Moore, whose time as Bond was still to come, prepares to take his horse for a morning ride around the Hollywood hills

Sean Connery gets his eye in as James Bond for some early publicity shots

wartime activities in Naval Intelligence and his travels around the world, have been reinterpreted at strategic moments in the novels; so much of Fleming himself is poured into Bond. It is therefore no wonder that he should have taken such an interest in the choice of the actor who was to play his alter ego.

In this regard the precise age of Bond was a major headache for the producers. If the novels were to be followed to the letter, the actor playing Bond had to look old enough to have seen wartime service, yet still be at the peak of his physical strength. Bond in the books is good-looking and sophisticated, yet extremely tough, and with a hefty drinking and smoking habit to boot. Even Fleming was obliged to shift the time-frame of Bond's life in later novels – which is just as well because otherwise, James Bond would now be approaching his 80th birthday, at the least. Fleming saw him as being experienced, but not that experienced.

Before *Dr No*, the producers cast their net wide in the hunt for the right Bond, perhaps aware that the success of the films would derive largely from finding the right face and body, as it were the right canvas onto which the complex characteristics of James Bond could be painted. Richard Burton, David Niven, George Baker (who later played the real Sir Hilary Bray in *On Her Majesty's Secret Service*) and a number of other very well-established British actors were considered. Niven, the archetypal upper-crust smoothie and a big crowd-puller, was a close friend of Fleming and was, significantly, his first choice for the part. Fleming also asked the veteran playwright and actor Noël Coward to play Dr No, but his telegrammed answer read: "To Dr No the answer is no no no no!"

Niven by then was already well into his fifties, and though he would have had no trouble playing the debonair sophisticate, he would have made an unconvincing tough, but did play the retired agent Sir James Bond in the 1967 *Casino Royale* spoof. Richard Burton, then at the height of his fame, had all the rough edges Niven lacked. Both these men were close to Fleming's notion of Bond as a seasoned veteran, old enough at times to be somewhat jaded and cynical about his profession. Strangely, at the same time, a still very young Roger Moore was also considered for 007. As it turned out he was unavailable due to commitments in his leading role in *The Saint* on British TV, and there was also a feeling that he was too young and too smooth. His time was still to come.

For Bond to work over several films, it was clear to Broccoli that he needed a man who could be groomed and moulded into the part, someone who would in the eyes of the cinema-going public not just play at, but actually be James Bond. Sean Connery, already known as "the truck driver" in Hollywood, where he had made a handful of

films, was certainly no public schoolboy. Elvis Presley had been a truck driver too, and Connery had the cruel good looks of the Bond of the books; he had all the edge which Broccoli would need and then some. Also, the British public were already in his favour; a newspaper poll in London had named him the ideal choice to play Bond long before his name came to the attention of the producers. But it remained to be seen if the Edinburgh trucky could be turned into the upper-class, suited hero of the novels.

It fell to Broccoli to perform the far from straightforward task of transforming him into 007, and creating a viable dress style for Bond was to be a large part of the challenge. Fleming had only sketched in a few details of Bond's wardrobe, but he was clearly a well-dressed man of some style. One of Fleming's most distinctive devices was the deployment of brand names, like smart bombs, throughout his texts, but, tantalizingly, he almost never does this in reference to Bond himself. With a journalist's fascination for lists and facts, and his own obsession with authenticity, Fleming might easily have made far more references than he does to Bond's wardrobe, to Jermyn Street, to Savile Row, to Italian tailors or Parisian shirtmakers. As a stylish man of the most precise tastes, Bond would assuredly have known as much about fine clothing as he did about champagne.

But Fleming appears deliberately to hold back from describing Bond's clothing in more detail – and happily, this very paucity of detail led to a pared-down image for Bond in the early films, with nothing superfluous, nothing overdesigned. Bond may personify a kind of aristocratic chic, and must always be well-dressed, but the more fashionably he dresses, the more he risks being cursed to style oblivion. Had he been a more flamboyant character his appeal might have waned as soon as fashion moved on. As it was it swiftly became apparent that Connery was the ideal choice, and Fleming professed himself delighted with it.

Other characteristics of Bond, the man, had also to be taken into account in styling him. Although in the Secret Service, Bond remained a commissioned officer in the Royal Navy. In the films he rarely appears in his own commander's uniform, but even in civilian attire he still has the military man's obsession with smartness. And his job, by its highly peripatetic nature, defines a severely restricted wardrobe. It would be inconceivable for Bond, leaving London at a few hours' notice, to be carrying an enormous suite of luggage.

Moreover, just like Fleming's, Bond's was a world of material certainties, not trunks full of choices. There was the right drink (vodka martini), the right cigarettes (Morland Specials), the right car (his supercharged $4\frac{1}{2}$-litre Bentley), the right length of time to cook a boiled egg (three and a third minutes) and even the right shampoo (Pinaud Elixir,

Bond, here with Kerim Bey in Istanbul in *From Russia With Love*, wears one of his new lightweight suits specially tailored for the film. Producer 'Cubby' Broccoli nominated this as his favourite Bond film as it was here that the Bond style began to be defined

(*Above, right*) George Lazenby in *On Her Majesty's Secret Service*, 1969. In the post-Carnaby Street era, interest in men's fashion was taking off in Britain, and the pronounced lapels and pocket flaps of his suit hint at styles to come

(*Left*) Sean Connery, returning to the role in *Diamonds Are Forever*, 1971, wears a wardrobe which shows a return to the restraint of the earlier films, although styles had changed in the nine years since *Dr No*: note the windsor knot, no pocket handkerchief and the widening of the pocket flaps and lapels

Live and Let Die, 1973, saw a new Bond and a very new Bond look: Roger Moore wears a contemporary safari-style suit, with slightly flared trousers and slip-on shoes

Roger Moore in *The Man with the Golden Gun*, 1974, wears a safari jacket with all the usual Bondian accessories

Roger Moore enjoyed the part which the wardrobe played in his characterization of Bond. Here he checks to see if his latest outfit is along the right lines – with an expert

(*Left*) Roger Moore has taken some flak for his Seventies styling; but in "the decade that style forgot", his look was comparatively restrained by the standards of, say, his hairdresser, whose flares, lapels and shirt collar went a great deal further

(*Above*) Roger Moore clowns around with a serious pair of sheers picked up from Doug Hayward's cutting-out bench. From a series of photographs by Terry O'Neil

(*Left*) Dennis Selinger, his agent, and Roger Moore select cloths with tailor Doug Hayward at his premises in Mount Street, Mayfair

Sean Connery's memorable beach encounter with Ursula Andress in *Dr No*. Connery's short-sleeved knitted shirt was to become a global casualwear classic over the next 30 years

referred to by Fleming somewhat overexcitedly as "that Prince of Shampoos"). Bond approaches the way he dresses with the same complete certainty. Things are either right or wrong. And that's that.

In fashion terms the spare modern clothing thrown up in the early Sixties has remained right far longer than the embryonic designer menswear of the Seventies. Although in many respects his clothing echoes the lean lines of Connery's Sinclair-cut suits, George Lazenby's 1969 suits already show signs of the wider lapels and more fashionable use of colour that would become the trademark of Roger Moore's Bond. In one memorable section of *On Her Majesty's Secret Service*, to the strains of Louis Armstrong's "We Have all the Time in the World", Lazenby goes through no less than six different outfits as he and Diana Rigg enjoy the romantic interlude in Lisbon which sets the scene for the tragic epilogue to the film: namely, riding kit with tweed jacket and sand-coloured silk stock, sky-blue double-vented single-breasted suit, blazer and grey flannel trousers, pink open-necked shirt, grey Prince of Wales check suit and finally a three-piece chalkstripe suit.

Style-wise, Lazenby was clearly a different animal from Connery and the notion of the wardrobe consisting only of classic essentials was already fading, pointing the way to the playboy image of Roger Moore's Bond. When Connery returned to the Bond stable briefly for *Diamonds Are Forever* in 1971, back too came the sparsely cut tailored suits and knitted ties. By then the fashion scene had changed and it was Lazenby's Bond rather than Connery's which Roger Moore inherited for *Live and Let Die*.

Moore, for his part, was no stranger to fashion, having designed much of his own clothing, and enjoyed a lavish billing to that effect in the final credits for the TV movie series *The Persuaders*. There, he and Tony Curtis co-starred as a pair of rich, party-animal playboys on the Med. For the upper-crust Moore, it was an easy step from this to playing Bond. At least, for the moment, he had age on his side – unlike the time when he was considered for the first Bond film – and by the Seventies, cinema audiences were demanding a softer approach. A new, fashion-conscious male had appeared, exemplified by a host of TV and cinema characters, and this shift was reflected in a sea change in Bond's wardrobe and style. For Moore glib lines seamlessly delivered in a safari shirt would be far more important assets than his fists.

The fashion business, which happily plunders the past with vulture-like enthusiasm, tends to look on the Seventies as "the decade that style forgot", preferring if anything to parody it, conveniently forgetting that the decade's greatest fashion excesses went hand in hand with the growth of fashion itself and the far wider accessibility of fashionable

(*Right*) Ian Fleming always felt that a visit to the set, here on *Dr No*, was an important occasion and dressed appropriately

(*Above*) No one has ever found more uses for towelling than James Bond. There are, however, limits to what can be done with the fabric – as they discovered in *Goldfinger*. Shirley Eaton and Ian Fleming discuss a solution

(*Right*) Englishmen of the time often knew very little about what to wear abroad. In *Thunderball*, Q makes just about every available sartorial mistake, but Bond is the honourable exception, comfortable and relaxed in open-necked, square-bottomed cotton shirt and matching trousers

Emilio Largo
(Adolfo Celi), the
best-dressed Bond
villain, exchanges
pleasantries with
Bond, in
Thunderball, 1965.
In the style stakes,
Bond keeps it
simple with a sea-
island cotton short-
sleeved shirt in
non-office stripes

The birth of the black-tie Bond, his most famous look. In *Dr No*, Connery wears the military-inspired narrow shawl-collared style, with the then-fashionable slim bow tie

clothing. His appearance may now seem extravagant, but Moore does no more in his films than Connery did in his, merely reflecting the tastes of his time. Even Moore's flared trousers and safari jackets fall far short of the overblown looks available to men in the Seventies. His wardrobe is a simple, understated version of the prevailing and often outrageous trends in menswear.

Society tailor Doug Hayward was entrusted with the suiting of Roger Moore, and confirms that, flares notwithstanding, his intention was never for Bond to appear outlandish. The guiding principle informing the making of suits for James Bond has always been the same:

"Keep them as classic as possible, as I believe that people will be watching James Bond films in 20 years. During the time that we were making clothes for Roger Moore, there were a lot of new styles and colours being promoted for men. I took a view, therefore, that we should keep noticeable details, such as turnback cuffs, to a minimum.

Fred Astaire could walk down the street today in a suit that was made for him in the Thirties and look fabulous. I have always borne that in mind when making clothes for films and I don't think I have ever done work for a film I am now embarrassed by."

If Bond remains our most enduring suited hero, his off-duty clothing is every bit as formulaic, and has contributed significantly to the Bond myth. Fleming's references to Bond's casual clothing centre more than anything on comfort, and although formal and casual are strictly divided, the same reduced approach to dressing applies to both. For sport, and for any occasion where a suit is not required, Bond opts every time for the same, simple unfussy looks which he prefers.

He is completely at home in his leisure clothing, anywhere in the world. Fleming's attachment to his home Goldeneye and the rest of the Caribbean shifted Bond's stylistic centre of gravity decisively away from his London base, and if Bond was to fetch up regularly in the Far East or the West Indies and preserve his unruffled appearance, his wardrobe must be able to cope with the tropics. Wherever possible Bond wears fabrics which are comfortable in the heat – sea-island cotton, raw silk, tropical worsted. In *Thunderball*, which would become Connery's fourth film, he is described thus:

"He was wearing a very dark blue lightweight single-breasted suit over a cream silk shirt and a black knitted silk tie. Despite the heat he looked cool and clean, and his only concession to the tropics appeared to be the black saddle-stitched sandals on his bare feet".

On his feet, even with a suit, Bond prefers comfort to traditionalism, opting for soft, unstructured moccasins or the black, saddle-stitched sandals as worn by Fleming

every day at Goldeneye while he concocted new dangers for 007 at his golden typewriter. Bond rarely opts for anything more fussy than a flat-hemmed cotton shirt, cotton trousers (never jeans) sandals and a waterproof watch. In *Dr No, Goldfinger* and *Thunderball* Bond's beach or poolside outfits are typical of a sophisticated Sixties holiday wardrobe. As with his formalwear Bond rarely wears anything more patterned than subtle ginghams, pale stripes and Vichy checks. Bond's elemental style is often emphasized by the brighter, brasher beach shirts of others and especially Felix Leiter with his batik prints in *Thunderball*.

Even in the field, Bond is able to set himself apart from his rather hidebound compatriots from station M. In *Thunderball*, Q meets up with Bond in Nassau to equip him with his latest gadgets. Here, Desmond Llewelyn is every bit the lily-skinned English boffin, uncomfortable in his beach print shirt, khaki drill shorts and desert boots. Bond cuts a far smoother figure in his square-cut open-necked brown shirt with patch pockets and matching slim fit trousers with ankle vents. His slip-on moccasins and straw hat echo the sharp golfing casuals in which he slugged it out on the links at the Royal St Marks in *Goldfinger*.

Such is his casualwear, but dressing for the occasion is an absolute must for Bond. He is never underdressed, except when pitched unpreparedly into a social event, as in *Dr No*, when after being captured at Crab Key by the villain's henchmen, his torn clothes are replaced with a navy raw silk Nehru-collared jacket and cream trousers, presumably from No's own wardrobe. It certainly isn't Bond. There is something decidedly quaint about the insistence of Bond, and for that matter his enemies, on observing the minutiae of dressing for dinner – but such stubborn adherence to foibles of this kind are part and parcel of the Bond ethos, even if they were already becoming dated 30 years ago.

Anachronism or not, James Bond's dinner suit is the single most recognizable item in his wardrobe and his most enduring trademark. Its consistent appearance in the Bond films constitutes an invaluable record of the evolution of the dinner suit, and few men have got as much use from their DJ as Bond. For three decades men have looked to no other role model on which to base their understanding of black tie. Like other ceremonial clothing, black tie is a marginal fashion discipline whose evolution has always been slower than men's style in general, but the Bond movies have thrown up a surprising variety of possibilities within an essentially narrow field.

Sean Connery's appearances in black tie tended to be fleeting, and largely confined to the casino, although these scenes are pivotal moments in most of the film plots. Casinos represented for Fleming the ultimate confirmation of the high life to which he was

(*Top left*) The most recognizable Bond image. Sean Connery in a publicity still for *From Russia with Love*, 1963, with turnback satin cuffs, the fashionably 'folded' white pocket handkerchief of the period and non-standard gun

(*Top right*) Timothy Dalton and Carey Lowell in *Licence To Kill*, 1989, by which time dinner suits were under the influence of the fashion designers and the "fits where it touches" looser look

(*Right*) 'Cubby' Broccoli clasps the script for *The Spy Who Loved Me*, 1977, next to a wide-lapelled Roger Moore in trademark Bondian pose and a little black-dressed Barbara Bach

(*Far left*) James Bond has worn white tuxedos more often than one might expect the British to do. Here, in *Goldfinger*, 1964, with peaked lapels, accessorized with a red carnation and black handgun

(*Left*) Pierce Brosnan renews the hand-tailored tradition in *GoldenEye*, 1995, by wearing a three-piece single-breasted Brioni dinner suit, with peak lapels and no vents. The bow tie has deepened once again, and the tucked-in silk pocket handkerchief is back

(*Opposite*) Goldfinger knew no limits in his quest for self-expression: the gold-lapelled Lurex tuxedo was perhaps his most heinous act of villainy

so attracted, the natural lair of the high-rolling hood and of James Bond, although the writer himself was rather more careful with his own money, preferring bridge to baccarat. Sean Connery's military inspired shawl-collared barathea suits with turnback satin-faced cuffs and covered buttons are quintessentially Sixties. Not surprisingly, it was Roger Moore who, as the most playboy-like incarnation of Bond, took to the tux with the greatest ease, giving it a starring role in all of his films. Timothy Dalton wore his dinner suits out of duty to the scripts, and it has fallen to Brosnan to convey the casino as a believable location to an audience who have perhaps never been futher removed from them and the glamour they represent – which he does with great panache.

For a Brit, Bond appears surprisingly often in a white tuxedo, which would still be considered slightly inappropriate at many British black tie events, as against the more usual black barathea. But just as with his suits, Bond's style is clearly swayed by the influence of the crucial American cinema market. It is also fair to remember that many of the locations in which he is expected to wear black tie are tropical. This is particularly the case with Roger Moore, who wore black and white in equal measure.

Perhaps oddly, considering Fleming, Bond and Connery all had Scots ancestry, Bond has worn a dress kilt in place of the usual jacket and trousers only once. Regret-

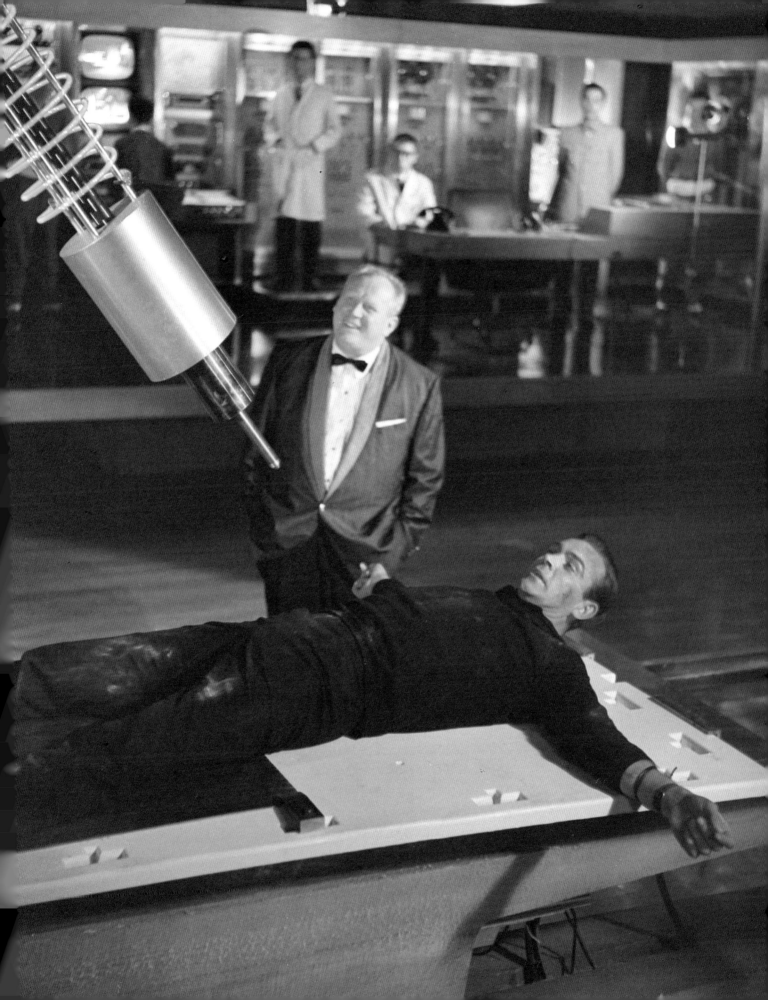

Joseph Wiseman is Dr No, sinister and perverse. His tunic with its high, stiff collar is reminiscent of a nineteenth-century Prussian uniform and has all its appeal

From Russia with Love had no prominent villain in funny clothes, but among the baddies, SPECTRE's Morzeny (Walter Gotell) looks menacing in black leather, as does Rosa Klebb (the great Lotte Lenya) in her prison wardress two-piece and sensible shoes

The villains' dress is carefully described in the books, perhaps none more so than Goldfinger's garish attire which was faithfully reproduced for the film.
In contrast, the golfing Bond sports the style which would become the golfer's norm, including an early logo-branded sweater

NICK SULLIVAN

Criminal catwalk and the best-dressed villain in town. In *Thunderball*
all the SPECTRE reps are dressed up for their Paris meeting, but none
more so than the immaculate Largo

150

(*Top left*) Donald Pleasence, as the fun-loving Blofeld in *You Only Live Twice*, 1967, favours the Mao collar for his tunic suit – so easygoing and comfortable for slouching around in

(*Top right*) Telly Savalas as Blofeld, with his only real friend, in *On Her Majesty's Secret Service*, 1969. Blofeld opts here for simple, traditional Bavarian costume with its stand-up collar, jetted breast pockets and decorative buttons, which were quite enough to convey megalomaniacal menace

(*Left*) *Diamonds Are Forever*, 1971, was the third film in succession to feature the cat-clutching arch-villain Ernst Stavro Blofeld. Charles Gray played him and his double with a chilling composure, opting again for the Chinese version of the tunic suit

In *Live and Let Die*, 1973, Roger Moore went up against Dr Kananga, Harlem's Mr Big and his sidekick, Tee Hee, both of whose penchant for blood red attire was in keeping with their taste for voodoo rituals

By 1974, casualwear for men had arrived and designers were experimenting feverishly with new fabrics and ideas. Scaramanga (Christopher Lee) in *The Man with the Golden Gun*, 1974, was an early fashion victim, choosing the comfort of a shirt-jacketed suit yet unable to surrender his conventional shirt and tie – obviously still *de rigueur* for world-class assassins

(*Right*) Curt Jürgens' Stromberg in *The Spy Who Loved Me* embraced the "leisure clothing" look of the day with evil glee. His overshirt top and matching trousers are the unacceptable face of 1977, but the studiously knotted silk stock suggests a man reaching back to an earlier age

(*Left*) Hugo Drax (Michael Lonsdale) in *Moonraker*, 1979, is plainly a fastidious man and no doubt went to Blofeld's tailor. He is another fan of the tunic, with its obvious advantages for the space age villain; no unnecessary ornamentation to get in the way of the electronic wizardry

tably, George Lazenby's Black Watch tartan, worn with black knee socks, sporran and ruffled lace jabot for *On Her Majesty's Secret Service*, is little more than another convenient vehicle for the *doubles senses* which inhabit the script. Lazenby's appearance in full Highland Dress is also at Piz Gloria, rather than in public, and while he is still assuming the role of Sir Hilary Bray. Although it remains a much-used alternative to the dinner suit for anyone with Scots connections, it is hard to imagine Connery retaining his cool image with cinema audiences while wearing a kilt.

If Ian Fleming rarely describes Bond's appearance he is far more forthcoming when it comes to his foes. In the novels and the films too, Bond's simplified, just-so dress system is emphasized by contrasting it with the peculiarities of dress preferred by his arch-enemies. Bond never discusses his own clothing, but he is quick to mete out swingeing observations on the sartorial shortcomings of his foes. Villains, in a word, dress badly. They are betrayed by their own fashion foibles as madmen, social climbers or both. Auric Goldfinger, of uncertain Baltic origin, made his millions from a string of jewellery shops and Bond makes a savage appraisal of his dress during their prophetic golf match.

"Goldfinger had made an attempt to look smart at golf and that is the only way of dressing that is incongruous on a links. Everything matched in a blaze of rust-coloured tweed from the buttoned golfer's cap centred on the huge flaming red hair, to the brilliantly polished, almost orange shoes. The plus-four suit was too well cut and the plus-fours themselves had been pressed down the sides. Everything about the man had grated on Bond's teeth from the moment he had seen him." In the film version, Bond's feelings are unspoken, but Goldfinger's ridiculous Wodehousian outfit is accurately rendered.

It is precisely at this moment Fleming disclaims any social snobbery on Bond's part, but it is clear that Fleming's own upbringing had given him a very definite view of his place and for that matter the place of others in the world – for example parvenues on golf courses. The clothes of the villains almost always serve to reiterate that Bond is a level above. As sales of the novels picked up, Fleming professed himself amazed as to who was actually buying his books, but he was surely being disingenuous: he could hardly have expected massive book sales to be generated only by those he perceived to be his own kind, and Fleming always hungered after a financial security and material luxury which eluded him for much of his life. It seems unlikely that the seductive ingredients of luxury and style which made James Bond the first male aspirational icon of the consumer age were not also calculated to make him appeal to those many book-buyers whose access to that style and luxury was in the way of being pure fantasy.

Whatever its motivations, one of the joys of the books is the way Fleming paints his sartorially preposterous villains, who will be let down as much by their vanity as by their megalomania. This can give the earlier Bond villains a somewhat two-dimensional quality, more like the supervillains of American comic strips than real-life baddies. But if Goldfinger and Blofeld are two-dimensional villains as wrong in their dress as Bond is right in his, Fleming is thankfully rather more expansive elsewhere. Bond and his enemies wisely show each other due deference before they try to kill each other. But only in one very significant case is Bond able genuinely to admire a villain's style.

Emilio Largo, so excellently played by Adolfo Celi in *Thunderball*, is not the top man but Blofeld's SPECTRE representative. Largo is a wealthy, well-dressed, sporting man. He has a slightly effeminate taste in expensive clothing – when we first meet him in the novel he is wearing a white sharkskin jacket and dabbing his brow with a Charvet handkerchief – yet Bond (and therefore Fleming too) clearly does not feel the same way about Largo as he does about Blofeld. As Blofeld's stooge, Largo will of course die, if only so that Blofeld can live, but on account of his style, neither Bond nor Fleming can dismiss him as being entirely evil:

"Emilio Largo, No 1, was a big, conspicuously handsome man of about 40. He was a Roman and he looked a Roman. In contrast to the hard, slow-moving brown eyes, the mouth with its thick, rather down-curled lips, belonged to a satyr. Ears that from dead in front looked almost pointed, added to an animalness that would devastate women".

In *Casino Royale*, Bond muses on the villain as his own alter ego. But only Largo really comes close. He is a nasty piece of work but he is also a businessman crook; as a professional rather than simply a madman, he has a detachment which mirrors Bond's own cynicism; he does not suffer the same withering hatred reserved by Bond for Blofeld and Fleming's other Hitlerian villains.

The supervillains themselves are always portrayed as having spent rather too much time and effort on their dress, often with a penchant for the Nehru- or Mao-collared suit that is both uniform-like (alluding to megalomanic tendencies) and quirky, suggesting, to Fleming at least, a slightly degenerate interest in their own appearance. Unwittingly these are the proto-fashion victims of the early Bond movies. Bond's simple, classic and by comparison, downright normal clothing is in perfect counterpoint to their idiosyncratic dress habits. Yet although this approach works well in more than half the films it is not consistently observed throughout.

In the Seventies and early Eighties, as Bond's wardrobe tended to reflect more closely the prevailing fashions, stylistic distinctions between Bond and his foes were far less obvious. Later Bond villains adopted the designer fashions of the Eighties, influenced by the prevailing Hollywood style movies of the day, such as *American Gigolo*, which not only catapulted Richard Gere to fame but his designer Giorgio Armani too. In *Licence To Kill*, drug baron Sanchez is the ideal Medellin/Miami smoothie, dressed down in pastel knits and flowing silk shirts. He may be every bit as much the psychotic killer as his predecessors, but Sanchez does look more normal, reflecting the more down-to-earth styling and plots of the Dalton incumbency.

By the time of the later Roger Moore and Timothy Dalton films, casual clothing had begun to influence the wardrobe of the hero as well as the villains. For Moore, the leather or suede blouson reflected the decisive shift in men's fashion during the Eighties. It also served to conceal Moore's by then slightly more than youthful appearance better than a tailored jacket would have done. Dalton, in his defence, took up the mantle of Bond at a time when the big-name fashion designers were encouraging men to dress down. Hollywood too was already turning away from the well-dressed hero to the reluct-

(*Below*) More casualwear began to appear in the Bond wardrobe in the Eighties. Roger Moore's blouson in *For Your Eyes Only*, 1981, marks a distinct shift in the outside world. Formal clothing was everywhere on the retreat and casual clothes could even be worn to work

(*Above*) Timothy Dalton's low-key wardrobe for *Licence To Kill*, 1989, was indicative of the no-rules, "Dress-down Friday" movement in menswear, as promoted by the men's designer labels

"If you paid as much attention to me as you do to your appearance, 007, I might just get something back in one piece", a resigned 'Q' (Desmond Llewelyn) might have been saying in *GoldenEye*

ant hero pitched unwittingly into life-threatening situations. The big box-office heroes – Sylvester Stallone, Bruce Willis, Arnold Schwarzenegger – left the villains to adopt the suit.

Timothy Dalton brought a certain edge to Bond, a taut, nervous style which was in fact close to Fleming's original treatment. But his clothes – largely his own eclectic choice from ready-to-wear shops – tended toward casual, designer-influenced ease. If the 60 Morlands and half-bottle of whisky a day were understandably missing from the Dalton films, his character was no less frayed at the edges for that. Stylishness remained a Bondian prerequisite, but Dalton looked uneasy in a suit, as he, like many men today, is obviously more comfortable in casual clothes. He injected gritty realism into the character – but really, the character has little to do with realism.

"James Bond is about so many ideas which are detached from most people's lives in a modern world," says Lindy Hemming, costume designer on *GoldenEye*. "But people expect him to go to casinos, meet gorgeous women and jump out of aeroplanes. People complained that Timothy Dalton's Bond looked too ordinary. They don't expect Bond to be like that, whereas they do expect it of Bruce Willis. They are different kinds of men. Willis is blue collar, Bond is very white collar."

In *GoldenEye*, Brosnan redresses the balance decisively in favour of well-tailored suits, a timely intervention as mens' fashion is now dictating a revival in looking smarter. Brosnan comes to the role with several advantages, one of which is that he is already a self-confessed lover of good clothes. As Hemming says, he has the perfect build for suits, one which even Sean Connery in his heyday would have found it difficult to match. To Brosnan, whose first cinema outing had been to see *Goldfinger*, the finely tailored three-piece suits which he wears so well in *GoldenEye* came with the territory.

ALL DRESSED UP

As the whole Bond film series is somewhat involved with the idea of sexual licence, it is hardly surprising that weddings are not a recurring theme. Bond's need to get out his formal dress is, therefore, somewhat limited, although when George Lazenby gets married to Diana Rigg, he chooses the local version, with its short black jacket, striped trousers, white shirt and silver tie.

The formal British morning dress is worn to good effect by M, Bond and Q in *A View to a Kill*, although as 'Royal Ascot' always takes place in June, it must have been exceptionally cold that year to explain the gloves. George Lazenby, impersonating Sir Hilary Bray, did not let Bond's Scottish ancestry down by cutting a fine figure in his full Highland evening dress – from his lace jabot down to his patent pumps. Timothy Dalton on the other hand obviously didn't make it to Moss Bros before flying out to Miami for Felix Leiter's wedding in *Licence to Kill*. His too-light grey morning suit, wing collar, striped ascot and 'cake-tin' topper must have been rented from a local shop, who probably wondered what on earth he had been up to when they got it back.

PEARL BUTTONS AND BOWS

The influence of the Bond films on contemporary men's fashion has not been studied in the same way as perhaps cars have. One only has to look to page 144 to where Nick Sullivan writes "For over three decades, men have looked to no other role model on which to base their understanding of black tie" to gauge the films' importance.

On inspection, James Bond's choice of soft-collared, soft-fronted dress shirts has remained remarkably consistent over the years – being mainly pleated fronts, with pearl buttons and only the occasional hint of a satin stripe or pale blue voile.

George Lazenby and Roger Moore both flirted with the frilled-front fashions of 1969 and 1973, and the wing-collar look of the last few years has never received the Bond seal of approval.

It was, however, left to the dimensional fluctuations of the simple black bow tie to illustrate just how much a staple item can be a powerless victim to the ever-changing demands of fashion.

The width remains fairly constant while the depth rises and falls, beginning with Sean Connery's 'Slim Jims' up to Roger Moore's velvet high of 1974, gradually shrinking back down to Timothy Dalton's restrained 1987 version, before deepening yet again for *GoldenEye*. Real aficionados of the 'Bow Tie Index' will be able to spot other variations dotted around the series, along with a wide variety of different lapel shapes and occasional satin turnback cuffs.

FIRST IMPRESSIONS

By the 1960s, traditional weighty overcoats were being challenged by new raincoats with warm quilted linings which could be "zipped in or zipped out", depending on the weather. Therefore the very traditional velvet-collared overcoat which Bond wears in *Dr No* over his dinner suit to go gambling at 'Le Cercle' in Park Lane was deliberately chosen to establish his cinema credentials as a traditionalist, just as the way he always throws his hat – when he still had one – onto the stand, signals his rebellious streak. George Lazenby took a step towards becoming a more modern man in a double-breasted car-coat. Roger Moore, on the other hand, reversed the process propelling his fitted Chesterfield overcoat, again with a velvet collar, into the fashion front line to counterpoint the current Harlem street style in *Live and Let Die*.

By the Dalton era, the overcoat had been banished altogether in favour of a green casual leather item which more closely reflected the 'designer' look of the times. Six years later though, the tailored overcoat had returned to favour – but without a velvet collar as yet – for Pierce Brosnan's trip north to St. Petersburg.

Pierce Brosnan chose a Brioni tailored three-piece suit for the pre-filming Press Conference at the Leavesdon Studio in January, 1995. Photographs of him with the famous DB5 sent out a clear signal that much of the traditional style of Bond would be in the new film. Martin Campbell, the director of *GoldenEye* – known for his action films – said "Bond has been on the screen for over 30 years and there are some things which you don't tamper with – one of which is his tailored suits"

FROM GOLDFINGER TO GOLDENEYE

Nick Sullivan

*A*s Sean Connery tails Goldfinger across Switzerland in his Aston Martin DB5, he wears narrow-cut, fawn cavalry twill trousers and a waisted two-button tweed "hacking" jacket with a single vent, over a white shirt and knitted tie. Thirty-odd years later, *GoldenEye* costume designer Lindy Hemming updated Connery's casual off-duty soldierly look for Pierce Brosnan in a way which is at once reminiscent of the early Sixties and perfectly right for the mid-Nineties: narrow-cut moleskin trousers, Church's brown semi-brogues, navy cashmere sweater, cornflower blue shirt and the nostalgic touch of a silk cravat.

Hemming was faced with the challenge of making sure that the wardrobe of Pierce Brosnan – and all the other players – was just right. It is clear that she considered the original Bond ethos carefully. "In the beginning the brief was very abstract, but I'd already made up my mind that what we wanted for the Nineties was to keep away from fashion. If you don't, in ten years time Bond's image might be in danger of looking rather washed-up. People tend to watch Bond films again and again – so it was important that he stayed close to the classic."

Something about the economy of line adopted by men during the first half of the Sixties *is* classic: it will always attract and be plundered by fashion designers, and the early Bond films starring Sean Connery are a valuable archive of this style of menswear. Much of what worked for Bond then, works well now too – it has been seen repeatedly in recent years, recreated and reworked, from the catwalk to the high street. Cross-pocketed trousers, three-quarter-length derivations of the Chesterfield and the covert coat, knitted ties, ankle boots and monk shoes, the ubiquitous three-button, single-breasted suit and even the sporty look of Sixties skiwear have all recently become key style items.

Thus it was to Sean Connery's Bond that Pierce Brosnan in *GoldenEye* would refer more than any other. "There was an unspoken consensus that the Connery films had a kind of energy that made them more durable than many of the others," says Hemming. "Somehow, the clothing rarely takes over. It lets you follow the action. In some of the later films, the costumes are so overstyled that they get in the way."

Terence Young, an ex-Irish Guards officer and the director of *Dr No*, *From Russia With Love* and
Thunderball was the man mainly responsible for setting the cinematic style of Bond.
Here, with Molly Peters on the set of *Thunderball*, he wears the shirt with the distinctive turnback
cuffs, which he introduced and which became part of Bond's wardrobe for all the early films

(*Opposite*) Sean Connery, with Daniela Bianchi, in
Istanbul for *From Russia With Love*, wears a suit
made for the film by Terence Young's tailor,
Anthony Sinclair, in a lightweight fabric of the kind
which Ian Fleming wore himself and approved

It was the first director, Terence Young, who before filming began on *Dr No*, took Sean Connery in hand and set out to create the pared down, unfussy wardrobe which became a trademark of the early films and set the style against which all subsequent Bonds would be judged. Young, an ex-army officer, who served in the Irish Guards during World War II and a stylish man himself, took Connery to his own tailor, Anthony Sinclair, who had premises in London's Conduit Street, just off Savile Row.

Although much of Bond's wardrobe certainly has a civilian dash to it, its restrained use of colour and its simplicity are consistent with a man who may be off-duty, undercover and in the Secret Service, but is still a naval officer. Sinclair judiciously gave Connery the fitted waist, longer jacket shape and narrower trousers favoured by military men. The knitted silk tie, square-tipped and unpatterned, in navy blue or black, is regularly mentioned in the novels, and features throughout the early Bond films.

Although he belonged to the Establishment, clearly a man as unique in the Secret Service as 007 had to be an individual too. Sinclair ensured that Bond's dress, neater and cleaner in line, stood out among his peers at station M. Bond's suits are deliberately sharper and lighter than the thicker, more lived-in looks of his colleagues. The more subtle Savile Row cut of Sinclair's outfits also emphasized the gentlemanly background of 007 and subliminally contributed to the success of the characterization.

(*Opposite*) No way to treat a suit… Jacques Boitier's throwing knife (almost) nails the 007 sleeve to the chimney-piece in *Thunderball*. Anthony Sinclair added a contemporary touch with the six-button, straight-cut "post-boy" waistcoat – a style then popularized by Jaeger for Men, and displayed prominently in their Regent Street window, just by Conduit Street, where Sinclair had his premises

(*Right*) Michael Fish, who went on to open his own shop 'Mr Fish', then still at Jermyn Street bespoke shirtmakers Turnbull & Asser, alters the sleeve of one of Sean Connery's 'signature' shirts, the ones with the turnback cuffs

(*Bottom*) The Savile Row tailors' trade paper *Tailor and Cutter* had some fun with early Bond publicity stills in a March 1965 issue

"YOU'LL GET YOUR MONEY WHEN YOU'VE DONE THE ALTERATIONS"

For shirts and ties, Connery was taken to Terence Young's own bespoke shirtmaker, Turnbull & Asser in Jermyn Street, and a signature shirt was assigned to James Bond, a vintage piece of Sixties-style design which appears extensively in the early films. 007's shirts had double cuffs, which were fastened underneath not with cuff links but with two pearl buttons; the cuff itself spreading away from the wrist like a shirt collar.

Although he is dressed expensively and well, Connery's suits were more sensible than modish, and his Bond is no dedicated follower of fashion. Anthony Sinclair was in every sense a classic tailor, yet he was known too for incorporating discreet fashionable details into his suits for his younger clientèle and did the same for Connery. In March 1965, he told the British tailoring trade bible, *Tailor and Cutter*, "I do not want anything of the fashion gimmick", at the same time stressing that although the suits he made were classic, this need not prevent him from incorporating the odd fashionable detail, in order to create for James Bond a modern version of the best in Savile Row tailoring.

Sinclair's minimal nods to the prevailing fashions included the occasional straight-bottomed waistcoat, narrow lapels with high notches and the ubiquitous Sixties-style turned-back satin cuffs on dinner jackets. The patterns used were mainly plain with the occasional small-scale Glen Urquhart and Prince of Wales checks.

Although it was Connery's precedent which Lindy Hemming chose to follow for her carefully considered styling of the mid-Nineties Bond, there was no question of turning him into a reprise of the Sixties: "James Bond has to be a classic man, not someone terribly interested in styles such as waistcoats which fasten two inches below the throat. He is still British and would therefore probably buy much of his clothing in the West End. Yet in modernizing him, and thinking why fewer men are wearing traditional suits, I looked into what was happening with traditional tailoring, but in lightweight construction."

The lightweight suit was an early staple in the Bond wardrobe. At a time when the day-to-day bespoke suit used fabrics significantly heavier than those of today, Ian Fleming's favourite was a navy blue, three-button, three-piece in lightweight worsted. His colleagues on *The Sunday Times* in Gray's Inn Road used to joke that the cloth was so thin that it would soon wear out and he would have to take the buttons back to his tailor (the London firm of Benson, Perry and Whitlow) to have a new suit sewn on. Whether this particular taste of Fleming's was influenced by his annual visits to Golden-eye, his home in Jamaica – the only place where he could write – or by his fascination with America, where lighter weights were already being worn, is unclear. But of those foibles of Fleming's dress sense which made the transition into Bond's screen wardrobe, the most important is certainly the lightweight suits.

(*Below*) George Lazenby in a publicity still for *On Her Majesty's Secret Service*, 1969, looks much smarter than the average Australian visitor of the day

(*Above*) The lightweight suit for overseas locations is a theme which threads right through the series. Here, admirers gaze at Roger Moore's "Continental look", a two-piece beige gaberdine suit, in *Octopussy*, 1983

(*Opposite*) Bond, in a lightweight three-piece suit suitable for warmer climates, enters the U.S.A. as a guest of Pussy Galore and Auric Goldfinger

UNE AVENTURE DE JAMES BOND

Ici commence un film-choc en huit épisodes : le célèbre agent secret James Bond vous dévoile les créations du prêt-à-porter anglais. Tous les modèles qu'il vous présente, vous les trouverez à Paris.

1

"M", chef du contre-espionnage anglais, a convoqué James Bond à son PC londonien de Regent's Park pour le charger d'une nouvelle mission.
Ian Fleming, auteur de la nouvelle "Entre chien et loup", joue le rôle de "M". Debout, á sa droite,

habillé par Daks (S. Simpson Ltd), dans un costume en peigné à petits carreaux gris ton sur ton, trois boutons, deux fentes, poche tickets, l'agent secret James Bond.

Voir prix et adresses, page 89.

Distribution :
"M" : Ian Fleming
James Bond : Hans Meyer
La Blonde : Celia Hammond
L'homme au cigare : Guy d'Arcangues
L'homme aux gants noirs : "Sweetie" Gatliff
Les joueurs : June Brunel
Joan Thring
Alec Murray
Le croupier : Monsieur X
Mis en scène et photographié
à Londres par : Helmut Newton
Armurerie : Cogswell and Harrison Ltd.

(*This page and opposite*) The French men's magazine *Adam* commissioned Helmut Newton in the early Sixties to interpret the "Bond look" using British menswear on sale in France at the time. They even persuaded Ian Fleming to play the part of M

JAMES BOND

2 Pour garder sa forme, James Bond fait un saut à 30 km de Londres, à Bisley, au champ de tir des services spéciaux. Entraînement obligatoire correspondant à la mission : abattre un dangereux agent ennemi. James Bond, "007" pour les initiés, appartient à la petite cohorte du "00", celle des agents autorisés à tuer. Dans la main gauche, il tient un pistolet Beretta 32 Walther PPK, dans la droite, un 38 spécial Smith and Wesson. Tenue appropriée : veste de tir et chasse "Blaley" à chevrons Irish tweed, chiné tabac et noir. Dos à soufflets, poches cartouches, cuir aux épaules, coudes et bas de manches. Pantalon golf assorti en même tissu ou bien, comme ici, en whipcord beige de Daks.

3 Détente ou préliminaire? Dans sa garçonnière de King's Road, flirt circonspect et prudent, James Bond ne sait pas si La Blonde est amie ou ennemie. Il a gardé son pistolet dans son holster, sous son cardigan Alan Paine de Godalming, de la main. champagne en poil de chameau grosse jauge, épaule "marteau", chemise Bonsoir en coton des îles Tattersall Checks (petits carreaux). Et La Blonde, pour ne pas être en reste, a son 22 Llama, crosse de nacre, à porté

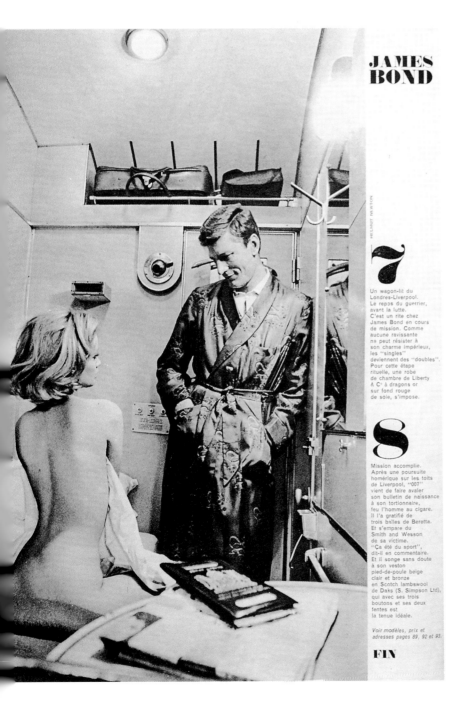

JAMES BOND

7 Un wagon-lit du Londres-Liverpool. Le repos du guerrier, avant la lutte. C'est un rite chez James Bond en cours de mission. Comme aucune ravissante ne peut résister à son charme impérieux, les "singles" deviennent des "doubles". Pour cette étape rituelle, une robe de chambre de Liberty & Cⁱᵉ à dragons or sur fond rouge de soie, s'impose.

8 Mission accomplie. Après une poursuite homérique sur les toits de Liverpool, "007" vient de faire avaler son bulletin de naissance à son tortionnaire, feu l'homme au cigare. Il l'a gratifié de trois balles de Beretta. Et s'empare du Smith and Wesson de sa victime. "Ça été du sport", dit-il en commentaire. Et il songe sans doute à son veston pied-de-poule beige clair et bronze en Scotch lambswool de Daks (S. Simpson Ltd), qui avec ses trois boutons et ses deux fentes est la tenue idéale.

Voir modèles, prix et adresses pages 89, 92 et 93.

FIN

(*Left and bottom left*) In France, the largest textile group of the time, Boussac launched ranges of raincoats, suits, shirts and towelling with this spoof letter sent to thousands of potential customers

Message personnel de JAMES BOND

JAMES
BOND
007

AUX ADEPTES

DU "NEW STANDING"

JAMES BOND 007

le QUELQUE PART 1965
EN MISSION

AU SERVICE DE
SA GRACIEUSE MAJESTÉ

•

Objet: LE "NEW STANDING"

Monsieur,

Ne vous méprenez pas sur les raisons qui m'ont fait prêter mon nom aux vêtements "New Standing" édités par les Ets BOUSSAC.

Une banale opération publicitaire ? Je serais navré que vous commettiez cette erreur. Pareil procédé n'est ni dans les habitudes des services secrets de Sa Gracieuse Majesté auxquels j'ai l'honneur d'appartenir, ni dans celles des Ets BOUSSAC. Simplement, ayant une certaine conception de l'art vestimentaire, j'ai saisi l'occasion qui m'était offerte de vous la faire partager.

D'abord, je veux être élégant. Faire le coup de poing avec les émissaires de Goldfinger ne me parait pas une excuse pour être aperçu en tenue négligée. Je suis horrifié par le style débraillé de tant de jeunes d'aujourd'hui.

Ensuite, j'ai le plus grand respect pour l'hygiène. Je m'agite beaucoup. Il me faut des vêtements en tissus légers, aérés et lavables, qui permettent au corps de respirer.

Et puis, bien sûr, j'aime mon confort. My goodness, marchons avec notre temps ! Partout, en avion, à l'hôtel, dans nos appartements, nous vivons sous le signe d'un confort grandissant. Notre garde-robe doit s'y adapter.

Enfin, je veux du pratique. Si vous aviez à loger dans une valise des poignards, un poste-émetteur, des bombes fumigènes, vous verriez ! Il me faut des vêtements très peu encombrants et qui, lavés le soir, soient le lendemain matin impeccables sans repassage ; je n'ai pas une minute à perdre.

Toutes ces qualités, je les ai trouvées dans les imperméables BLIZZAND, les costumes en Tergal BOUSSAC, les chemises NOVELTEX, les articles en éponge JALLA, qui constituent le "New Standing James BOND" créé sous mon nom par les Ets BOUSSAC.

Voilà pourquoi j'ai accepté d'en être le parrain. Voilà pourquoi je vous félicite de votre bon goût : avec l'espoir qu'ayant goûté au "New Standing James BOND", vous en deviendrez les adeptes fidèles.

James Bond

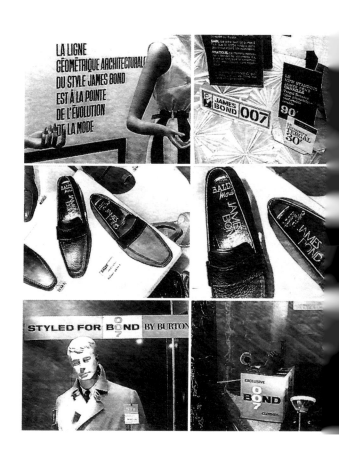

Tailor and MEN'S WEAR, October, 1965

Pelaco triggers off the Shirt with a Licence to Thrill!

JAMES BOND 007
BY PELACO

☞ WARNING: INFRINGERS WILL
BE PROMPTLY GOLD-FINGERED!

Pelaco holds the exclusive Australian licence to manu-
facture and market this shirt, and any infringers will
be promptly Gold-Fingered. Only ONE James Bond 007
Shirt may be made, and it will be made by Pelaco.

In pure silk and 'Terylene' . . . the most luxurious shirt in history!
Named after the Man with the Licence to Kill, James Bond 007
by Pelaco is tailored from a rich blend of pure imported Silk and
fine 'Terylene'. Like its famous namesake, James Bond 007 by
Pelaco will withstand any amount of karate, judo and pressing
engagements with boudoir blondes. A choice of latest collar styles,
and high fashion colours.
World-wide publicity has already pre-sold customers on James
Bond 007. Pelaco will back your sales with full page ads. in daily
press throughout Australia, with vibrant point of sale posters, with
dramatic shirt packaging. Pelaco's faster turnover means no
stock risk, no dust-gathering, no profit-cutting markdowns. Fast
in-stock service, and 60 to 70 days credit, mean you outlay virtually
no capital in stock, while you make the most profit.

(*Left and below*) Two advertisements for ranges
of James Bond, 007 men's shirts and suits,
which were on sale in Australia, around 1965

His signature.   Ours.

The James Bond 007 suit.

Who's the mastermind behind this sensational coup?
Who else but Ernest Hiller. His, is the only company
licensed to cut it. What's it like? Try thinking about
how a traditional English suit should look. Got
the picture? Now, to add the James Bond flair, let's
get rid of the old stiff-upper-lip and get with it. The
result? A suit that deftly combines the best of the
British style with such racy features as: a slightly
flared waist; four buttons on the sleeve; a ticket
pocket; a suave new lining; plus a dashing collection
of pure wool fabrics in solids and checks.
Confidentially . . . with all the publicity Mr. Bond is
getting these days, and with our own national newspaper advertising, your next assignment should be
an order. A sales-winning order we mean. One of our
agents would love to fill you in with the whole story.

Ernest Hiller

JB18

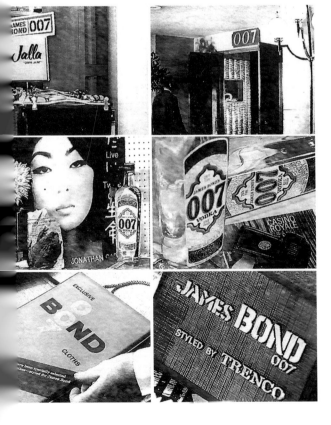

(*Left*) Many manufacturers from all over the
world, particularly those in menswear and
the drinks market, sought licences to label
their products '007' or 'James Bond'

Brioni were the tailors of choice for Hollywood luminaries visiting Rome in the Fifties and Sixties. Among others to stand to attention for the master tailors were Henry Fonda, John Wayne, Clark Gable and Anthony Quinn

(*Opposite*) Checchino Fonticoli, Brioni's master tailor fits Pierce Brosnan with one of his suits

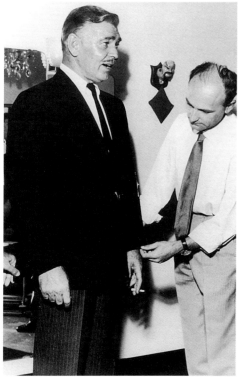

A publicity still for *GoldenEye*. Pierce Brosnan and an elegant Izabella Scorupco, who, as Natalya, spends much of the film in the same cardigan and skirt – the expensive clothes being worn by Xenia, the villainess with access to Russian mafia money

It was thus fitting that Hemming's investigations should lead her to the door of the Roman bespoke house Brioni, whose pioneering work in tailoring lightweight cloths was a telling factor in her choice and one reason, despite jingoistic objections, why Savile Row was not chosen by her. "I wanted a company which was capable of tailoring in the Savile Row manner, and – because of *GoldenEye*'s tight shooting schedule – could produce a lot of suits very quickly", she explains.

Jonathan Lipman, production director at Angels & Bermans (London's world-famous costumiers, who have *inter alia* been involved in every Bond production except the Dalton films) concurs: "The brief was not to have Bond stuck in Savile Row, but to use Savile Row style with Italian influences: a softer line but with the severity of the original". Hence the choice of the Roman tailors – although Brioni's ability to deliver the sheer luxury element was a factor too. Hemming says she wanted "something that was unmistakably synonymous with expensiveness. This man must look immaculate, not strange or foppish or too fashionable."

Fifty years old in 1995, Brioni has been tailoring fine clothing for a select band of high-fliers since its inception. In the 1950s the firm was a leading light in the group of Roman tailors, who for the first time combined exquisite lightweight tailoring with progressive fashion ideas and set the scene for the growth of Italian fashion as the world force in menswear. Brioni became the favourites of the original Mediterranean jet set: Italy's leading actors, working out of Rome's Cinecittà, plus visiting Hollywood stars such as Clark Gable, John Wayne, Gary Cooper and Henry Fonda. Today, the firm employs 800 tailors and seamstresses in their workshop factory in the Abruzzi region overlooking the Adriatic. From there they ship out 250 hand-made suits every day to 300 of the world's most exclusive menswear shops and stores whose customers' lists for Brioni suits read like an international *Who's Who* of business, politics, royalty and the arts.

It is appropriate to the international confidence given by Ian Fleming to Bond that he should be familiar with the best tailoring available. The choice of tailor also reflects a longstanding Continental love for all things Bondian and the mutual respect – as well as rivalry – between the premier tailors of England and Italy. Indeed, the historical roots of the "Abruzzese school" – whose members include some of the very best tailors in Italy, Caraceni, Ciro Giuliano and Brioni's co-founder Nazareno Fonticoli – are to be found in Britain. When Sir Paolo Tosti, composer and singing master to the court of Edward VII, at the turn of the century, sent his old Savile Row suits home for his relatives in Abruzzi to wear, local tailors took them apart stitch by stich to learn their secrets.

Umberto Angeloni of Brioni recalls the early days of 007 in Europe: "In both France and Italy the books did not stir much interest with the general public, and it wasn't until the first couple of films that the character gained momentum, around 1964. Then, especially in France, menswear after the style of Bond virtually generated an industry of its own: Boussac, France's most important textile group, created a line of Bond rain-coats, shirts, and pyjamas, both for men, bearing the 007 number and also for boys with the number $003\frac{1}{2}$. One style boasted twenty-four secret pockets! In Paris, the Galeries Lafayette department store opened a 'Boutique James Bond', Printemps did the same, and custom tailor Bayard presented four 'James Bond' models, all with waist-coats. Enthusiasm reached a peak in 1965 when over 6,000 shops in France stocked licensed James Bond products, including clothes for men and women, jewellery, acces-sories and cameras."

In Italy, Bond's success was equally impressive, but did not result in the same kind of commercial exploitation. Italian tailors were not especially impressed by Bond's style; Caraceni decreeing that, in his opinion, it was "a bit vulgar, in the American way and definitely dubious according to the Italian canons of elegance." The most disturbing and telling points were the sandals with the suit, and the dreadful British habit of only ever wearing short socks.

Like Connery, Brosnan's Bond wears just a select few stylish, but formally tailored outfits – six in all, including his dinner jacket and blazer. Each outfit had to be supplied in differing quantities depending on the scene – more than 30 suits being destroyed dur-ing filming of the action sequences. For his arrival in St Petersburg, he eschews casual, comfortable clothes of the kind favoured by most air travellers nowadays, choosing instead an elegant look, redolent of the more glamorous days of air travel: a worsted three-piece grey suit with faint blue windowpane overcheck, full-length navy cashmere and wool overcoat, a white shirt and woven silk tie. The result is typical of his new style: considerably smarter and more conservative than that of his immediate predecessors.

Brosnan, a boyhood fan of Bond, plainly enjoys his role in updating the myth and sees 007's style as crucial: "The wardrobe is an essential part of playing James Bond," he says, "Putting on the right suit should make the actor look, move and behave with a cer-tain style. When I wasn't wearing a suit, it was more difficult to feel like James Bond."

Although Lindy Hemming based Bond's new wardrobe on a classic framework, she set out to reflect the current fashion mood too, just as Anthony Sinclair had done before. "When I went first over to Brioni to work on Pierce's wardrobe, we discussed style and proportion and came up with a very modern jacket shape; although classic, it is slightly

In the Carribbean, with Natalya (Izabella Scorupco) and a BMW Z3
Roadster, a tieless, more relaxed 1995 James Bond still chooses to
wear a suit – although by now it is an ultra lightweight one which
Fleming would have envied

(*Left*) The Glencheck suit has been another Bond staple since the early days. Pierce Brosnan's Brioni version, a two-piece brown Saxony, was what he chose for his latest visit to the office of Judi Dench's M

(*Opposite*) Pierce Brosnan, on one of the *GoldenEye* sets, photographed by John Stoddart, in a style reminiscent of the studio portraits of the Forties and Fifties stars

A publicity still for *GoldenEye*, in which Bond, having demolished part of St Petersburg in a borrowed T-55 tank, still finds time to straighten his tie

longer and looks good with three buttons as well as two. I also wanted to incorporate traditional details such as ticket pockets which would suggest that the clothing might have come from Savile Row, properly finished cuff buttonholes and a hand-finished look to the garment as a whole. The silhouette of the jacket required quite a narrow trouser to balance it, so it was important to choose shoes with the right look and weight, which I was able to do from Church's ranges."

Brioni worked closely with Lindy Hemming, sending master tailor Checchino Fonticoli and his assistant to London on various occasions, to develop the final model. The result are classic suits, with a natural but fitted shoulder line, which project an image of international elegance and a strong masculine identity. As Hemming says "Brioni helped me achieve my aim for Bond – of distinction without distraction."

What then helped Brioni to successfully out-Savile Row Savile Row in their suiting of James Bond? Angeloni again: "This was a major challenge: to interpret and define the style of the best known screen hero in the world. It is said that over half of the world's population has seen a James Bond film and more people would recognize 007 than Superman. It was a major responsibility too: costume was again going to be an important element in the delicate task of relaunching Bond six years after a sartorially weak interpretation by Dalton. It finally proved to be a great opportunity to convey an important message: that one can still look powerful, youthful and sexy in tailored clothing. The immediate acceptance of the new tailored Bond at the box office by both the older fans and the crucial younger market, probably heralds a turning point for the menswear industry."

There is already a feeling that with Brosnan and *GoldenEye*, the circle has been closed and much of the original James Bond is back. Interest in the film has been phenomenal, similarly ticket sales, suggesting that the forces at play have to do with more than just excitement at a new action movie. The world, it seems, is bored of dressing down and ready for a touch of elegance once again. Mens' fashion in general, is more of a force at large than it has been at any time since the Sixties; newspapers everywhere are carrying expanded style sections and, while the timeless classic looks of the early Sixties have a part to play, this is not a retrograde step – nostalgia for the Fifties, Sixties, Seventies being in itself a slightly dated, directionless, Eighties concept. Rather, the early Sixties and mid-Nineties, the worlds reflected in *Goldfinger* and *GoldenEye* respectively, share a deep longing for real glamour, style, elegance, and the character who satisfies this longing best, the classic personification of the suited hero, has never looked better. His name – as everyone, everywhere, knows – is still James Bond.

APPENDICES

THE JAMES BOND BOOKS

Casino Royale (1953)

Live and Let Die (1954)

Moonraker (1955)

Diamonds Are Forever (1956)

From Russia With Love (1957)

Dr. No (1958)

Goldfinger (1959)

For Your Eyes Only (1960) *short stories*

Thunderball (1961)

The Spy Who Loved Me (1962)

On Her Majesty's Secret Service (1963)

You Only Live Twice (1964)

The Man with the Golden Gun (1965)

Octopussy (1966) *short stories*

THE OFFICIAL JAMES BOND FILMS

Title	Starring	Directed by
Dr. No (1962)	*Sean Connery*	*Terence Young*
From Russia With Love (1963)	*Sean Connery*	*Terence Young*
Goldfinger (1964)	*Sean Connery*	*Guy Hamilton*
Thunderball (1965)	*Sean Connery*	*Terence Young*
You Only Live Twice (1967)	*Sean Connery*	*Lewis Gilbert*
On Her Majesty's Secret Service (1969)	*George Lazenby*	*Peter Hunt*
Diamonds Are Forever (1971)	*Sean Connery*	*Guy Hamilton*
Live And Let Die (1973)	*Roger Moore*	*Guy Hamilton*
The Man with the Golden Gun (1974)	*Roger Moore*	*Guy Hamilton*
The Spy Who Loved Me (1977)	*Roger Moore*	*Lewis Gilbert*
Moonraker (1979)	*Roger Moore*	*Lewis Gilbert*
For Your Eyes Only (1981)	*Roger Moore*	*John Glen*
Octopussy (1983)	*Roger Moore*	*John Glen*
A View To A Kill (1985)	*Roger Moore*	*John Glen*
The Living Daylights (1987)	*Timothy Dalton*	*John Glen*
Licence To Kill (1989)	*Timothy Dalton*	*John Glen*
GoldenEye (1995)	*Pierce Brosnan*	*Martin Campbell*

THE BOND VILLAINS

Joseph Wiseman	as *Dr. Julius*	in *Dr. No*
Gert Frobe	as *Auric Goldfinger*	in *Goldfinger*
Adolfo Celi	as *Emilio Largo*	in *Thunderball*
Donald Pleasence	as *Ernst Stavro Blofeld*	in *You Only Live Twice*
Telly Savalas	as *Ernst Stavro Blofeld*	in *On Her Majesty's Secret Service*
Charles Gray	as *Ernst Stavro Blofeld*	in *Diamonds Are Forever*
Yaphet Kotto	as *Mr. Big/Dr. Kananga*	in *Live And Let Die*
Christopher Lee	as *Scaramanga*	in *The Man with the Golden Gun*
Curt Jurgens	as *Stromberg*	in *The Spy Who Loved Me*
Michael Lonsdale	as *Hugo Drax*	in *Moonraker*
Julian Glover	as *Kristatos*	in *For Your Eyes Only*
Louis Jourdan	as *Prince Kamal Khan*	in *Octopussy*
Christopher Walken	as *Max Zorin*	in *A View To A Kill*
Joe Don Baker	as *Whitaker*	in *The Living Daylights*
Jeroen Krabbe	as *Koskov*	in *The Living Daylights*
Robert Davi	as *Franz Sanchez*	in *Licence To Kill*
Sean Bean	as *Alec Trevelyan*	in *GoldenEye*

THE BOND WOMEN

Ursula Andress	as *Honey Ryder*	in *Dr. No*
Daniela Bianchi	as *Tatiana Romanova*	in *From Russia With Love*
Honor Blackman	as *Pussy Galore*	in *Goldfinger*
Claudine Auger	as *Domino*	in *Thunderball*
Mie Hama	as *Kissy Suzuki*	in *You Only Live Twice*
Diana Rigg	as *Tracy Vicenzo*	in *On Her Majesty's Secret Service*
Jill St. John	as *Tiffany Case*	in *Diamonds Are Forever*
Jane Seymour	as *Solitaire*	in *Live And Let Die*
Britt Ekland	as *Mary Goodnight*	in *The Man with the Golden Gun*
Barbara Bach	as *Major Anya Amasova*	in *The Spy Who Loved Me*
Lois Chiles	as *Holly Goodhead*	in *Moonraker*
Carole Bouquet	as *Melina Havelock*	in *For Your Eyes Only*
Maud Adams	as *Octopussy*	in *Octopussy*
Tanya Roberts	as *Stacey Sutton*	in *A View To A Kill*
Maryam D'Abo	as *Kara Milovy*	in *The Living Daylights*
Carey Lowell	as *Pam Bouvier*	in *Licence To Kill*
Izabella Scorupco	as *Natalya*	in *GoldenEye*

JAMES BOND'S STYLE MAKERS

Dr. No	*Tessa Welborn* Costume Designer
From Russia with Love	*Jocelyn Rickards* Costume Designer
Goldfinger	*Elsa Fennell* Wardrobe Supervisor
Thunderball	*Anthony Mendleson* Costume Designer
You Only Live Twice	*Eileen Sullivan* Wardrobe Supervisor
On Her Majesty's Secret Service	*Marjory Cornelius* Costume Designer
Diamonds Are Forever	*Elsa Fennell, Ted Tetrick* Wardrobe Supervisors
Live and Let Die	*Julie Harris* Costume Designer
The Man with the Golden Gun	*Elsa Fennell* Wardrobe Supervisor
The Spy Who Loved Me	*Ronald Paterson* Fashion Consultant
	Rosemary Burrows Wardrobe Supervisor
Moonraker	*Jacques Fonteray* Costume Designer
For Your Eyes Only	*Elizabeth Waller* Costume Designer
Octopussy	*Emma Porteous* Costume Designer
A View to a Kill	*Emma Porteous* Costume Designer
Licence To Kill	*Jodie Tillen* Costume Designer
GoldenEye	*Lindy Hemming* Costume Designer

THE JAMES BOND FILMS FEATURED IN THIS VOLUME

t – top; *tl* = top left; *tr* = top right; *l* = left; *r* = right;
b = bottom; *bl* = bottom left; *br* = bottom right

Dr No: 14, 15, 21*b*, 126, 139, 143, 148*l*, 164*t*

From Russia With Love: 21*t*, 33, 70, 90*bl*, 124*tr*, 133*tl*, 148*r*, 162*tr*, 169

Goldfinger: 25, 68, 69, 82, 90*tr*, 118*br*, 120*tr*, 120*bl*, 146*l*, 147, 149, 162*br*, 175, 177

Thunderball: 28, 29, 53, 71, 75*tr*, 76, 89*bl*, 89*br*, 122*tr*, 122*b*, 124*br*, 140*br*, 141, 150, 172

You Only Live Twice: 34*t*, 34*b*, 49*tl*, 73, 87*tl*, 87*bl*, 125*bl*, 151*tl*

On Her Majesty's Secret Service: 86*b*, 88*tr*, 91*tl*, 118*tr*, 119*bl*, 133*tr*, 151*tr*, 160*tr*, 161*l*, 163*bl*, 165*tl*, 176*l*

Diamonds Are Forever: 133*b*, 151*b*

Live and Let Die: 91*tr*, 91*br*, 134, 152*r*, 164*b*

The Man with the Golden Gun: 90*br*, 121*br*, 123*tr*, 125*tl*, 135, 152*l*, 163*tl*

The Spy Who Loved Me: 61, 87*r*, 89*tl*, 89*tr*, 125*tr*, 153*t*

Moonraker: 35*t*, 35*b*, 55*b*, 119*tl*, 120*br*, 123*bl*, 153*b*

For Your Eyes Only: 88*br*, 157*l*

Octopussy: 176*r*

A View To A Kill: 121*tl*, 160*b*

The Living Daylights: 86*t*, 119*tr*, 121*tr*, 165*bl*

Licence to Kill: 155, 157*r*, 161*tr*, 161*br*

GoldenEye: 116, 123*br*, 146*r*, 158, 163*tr*, 165*r*, 187, 188, 191

PICTURE CREDITS

t = top; *tl* = top left; *tc* = top centre; *tr* = top right; *l* = left; *r*= right; *c* = centre
b = bottom; *bl* = bottom left; *br* = bottom right

Adam Magazine: 178, 179*tr*, 179*br*, 179*bl*
Advertising Archives: 26*l*, 30*r*, 31*tl*, 31*r*, 31*bl*
Brioni Archive: 182*tl*, 182*tr*, 182*bl*, 182*br*, 183
Condé Nast Publications: 26*r*
EON Productions Archive: 12, 14, 15, 19, 21*t*, 21*b*, 23, 25, 27, 28, 29, 33, 34*t*, 34*b*, 35*t*, 35*b*, 41, 49*tl*, 53,
    55*b*, 61, 68, 70, 71, 73, 75*tr*, 76, 77, 82, 83, 86*t*, 86*b*, 87*tl*, 87*r*, 87*bl*, 88*tr*, 88*br*, 89*tl*, 89*tr*, 89*bl*, 89*br*,
    90*tr*, 90*bl*, 90*br*, 91*tl*, 91*tr*, 91*br*, 116, 119*tl*, 119*tr*, 120*bl*, 120*br*, 121*tl*, 121*br*, 122*tr*, 122*b*, 123*tr*, 123*br*,
    123*bl*, 124*tr* 124*br*, 125*tl*, 125*tr*, 125*bl*, 126, 129, 133*bl*, 134, 137*tl*, 139, 140*tr*, 140*l*, 140*br*, 141, 143,
    145*tl*, 145*tr*, 145*br*, 146*tr*, 147, 148*l*, 148*r*, 149, 150, 151*tl*, 151*tr*, 151*b*, 152*l*, 153*t*, 153*b*, 155, 157*l*,
    158, 160*tr*, 160*b*, 161*l*, 161*br*, 162*b*, 163*tl*, 163*tr*, 163*bl*, 163*br*, 164*t*, 164*b*, 165*tl*, 165*r*, 165*bl*, 166, 169,
    172, 175, 176*bl*, 176*tr*, 177, 185, 187, 188, 191
Express Newspapers/John McLusky: 79*tl*, 79*bl*, 79*br*, 81*t*, 81*c*, 81*b*
Filmarchiv, Dr. Siegfried Tesche: 170, 173*t*, 180*tl* (photo by Christian Storz for Playboy), 180*tc*, 180*bl*, 180*br*
Hulton Deutsch: 3, 10, 18*bl*, 18*br*, 45, 46, 47, 48*t*, 49*r*, 49*bl*, 55*t*, 58, 59, 60*tl*, 60*tr*, 60*b*, 66*tl*, 67, 75*tl*, 128*tr*,
    128*b*, 131
The James Bond 007 Fan Club Archive: 69, 78*bl*, 78*br*, 90*c*, 118*tr*, 118*br*, 119*bl*, 120*tr*, 121*tr*, 133*tl*, 133*tr*,
    135, 146*tl*, 152*r*, 157*r*, 161*tr*, 162*t*, 171
The Kobal Collection: 16*tr*, 74*tl*, 92, 94*tl*, 95, 97, 98, 99, 100*tl*, 100*r*, 100*bl*, 101, 102, 103, 105*tr*, 105*bl*, 108,
    109*tl*, 109*br*, 111, 112*t*, 112*b*, 113, 115, 128*tl*
Malcolm Lewis: 52
Magnum Photos Ltd: 18*t*/Cornell Capa, 38/George Rodger, 42/Henri Cartier-Bresson, 48*b*/Ian Berry,
    50/Henri Cartier-Bresson, 51/Dennis Stock, 56/Bruce Davidson, 64/Ian Berry, 66*tr*/Cornell Capa
Moviestore Collection: 74*tr*, 94*bl*, 104, 106
Terry O'Neil: 136, 137*tr*, 137*b*
Paramount Pictures: 114
Retro Video, London: 78*t*
Rex Features Ltd: 16*tl*, 17*tl*, 17*tr*, 94*r*, 168
The Ronald Grant Archive: 16*b*, 20*tl*, 20*tr*
Scope Features: 84
John Stoddart: 119*br*, 125*br*, 189
Tailor & Cutter: 173*b*
Tailor and Men's Wear, 181*tl*, 181*tr*
Town Magazine: 30*l*

The publishers would like to thank all those who have lent material for use in this book. Efforts have been
made to trace copyright holders. Should there be any omissions, the publishers will be pleased to rectify them
in an appropriate way.